Main Idea Activit
English Language I
and Special-Needs Students
with Answer Key

(HOLT)

Civics

HOLT, RINEHART AND WINSTON

A Harcourt Education Company

Austin • Orlando • Chicago • New York • Toronto • London • San Diego

Printed in the United States of America

ISBN 0-03-038714-0
1 2 3 4 5 6 7 8 9 082 07 06 05 04

Contents

Main Idea Activities

CHAPTER 1

Main Idea Activities 1.1

We the People

VOCABULARY Some terms to understand:

- **originated (p. 3):** began
- **adopted (p. 3):** took on or accepted
- **exercise (p. 3):** to apply or to put into effect
- **ideals (p. 4):** perfect models
- **heritage (p. 4):** tradition
- **just (p. 5):** reasonable
- **terms (p. 5):** length of time one serves in office
- **resources (p. 6):** possessions or assests
- **conscience (p. 6):** sense of right or wrong
- **principle (p. 7):** belief
- **economic (p. 7):** financial or dealing with money

ORGANIZING INFORMATION Complete the graphic organizer below. Use it to identify the roles and qualities of a good U.S. citizen.

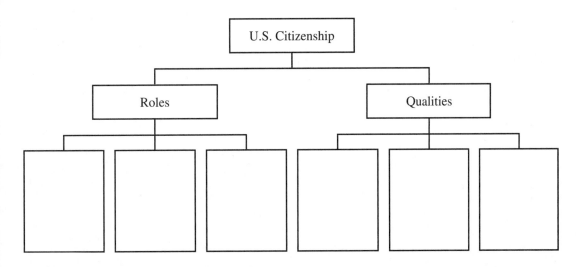

EVALUATING INFORMATION Mark each statement *T* if it is true or *F* if it is false.

_____ **1.** Civics is the study of what it means to be a Roman citizen only.

_____ **2.** The U.S. government is based on the ideals of freedom and equality.

_____ **3.** Under the U.S. form of government, the people rule through the officials they elect.

_____ **4.** Officials cannot be removed from office once they are elected by the people.

Chapter 1, Main Idea Activities 1.1, continued

_____ **5.** The study of civics helps you learn your role in government.

_____ **6.** Good citizens respect individual differences and take an active part in their government.

_____ **7.** The study of civics involves learning about the U.S. economic system.

_____ **8.** It is not the responsibility of state and local governments to provide free public schools for all young citizens.

_____ **9.** Being a U.S. citizen includes being a productive and sharing member of society.

_____**10.** The U.S. government does not yet guarantee that all persons qualified for a job have an equal opportunity to secure it.

REVIEWING FACTS Choose the correct terms from the following list to complete the statements below.

civics   heritage
citizen   resources
government

1. We must use our natural _____ wisely.

2. _____ is the organizations, institutions, and individuals who exercise authority as a political unit over a group of people.

3. The United States has a _____ of liberty and freedom.

4. The word _____ originated in ancient Greece.

5. A _____ is a legally recognized member of the United States.

CHAPTER  **1**

Main Idea Activities 1.2

We the People

VOCABULARY Some terms to understand:

- **descendants (p. 8):** children, grandchildren, great-grandchildren, etc.
- **origin (p. 8):** source or starting point
- **bondage (p. 9):** being dominated by another
- **policy (p. 9):** guideline or rule
- **wages (p. 10):** salary or income
- **restrictions (p. 10):** limits
- **cap (p. 10):** limit or top
- **persecution (p. 10):** prejudice or discrimination
- **authority (p. 11):** power
- **agency (p. 11):** group or organization
- **register (p. 11):** to record or to document
- **resent (p. 12):** to dislike
- **bar (p. 12):** to prevent or restrict
- **allegiance (p. 13):** loyalty

EVALUATING INFORMATION Mark each statement *T* if it is true or *F* if it is false.

_____ **1.** Many archeologists believe that the first people to settle in North America came from Africa.

_____ **2.** In 1492 Christopher Columbus sailed to the Americas and claimed land for Italy.

_____ **3.** Many Africans came to the Americas as slaves.

_____ **4.** In the 1920s, the United States established quotas for how many immigrants could come from a particular country or region.

_____ **5.** If you are born in the United States, you are automatically a citizen.

_____ **6.** If one or both of your parents were U.S. citizens, you are also a citizen by birth.

_____ **7.** The government cannot force aliens to leave the United States, even if they violate a law.

_____ **8.** Aliens may vote, but they cannot hold public office.

_____ **9.** In order to be naturalized, aliens must prove that they can read, write, and speak English.

Chapter 1, Main Idea Activities 1.2, continued

REVIEWING FACTS Choose the correct terms from the following list to complete the statements below.

immigrant   native-born citizen   refugees
quotas   deport
aliens   naturalization

1. _____ are people living in the United States who are citizens of another country.

2. An alien may become a citizen through a legal process called

_____.

3. The United States used to set _____ on how many immigrants could come into the country.

4. People who flee persecution in their home countries are called

_____.

5. A(n) _____ is a person who came to the United States from other lands.

6. If you are born in any U.S. state or territory, you automatically become a(n)

_____.

7. The government can _____ aliens if they violate the law.

UNDERSTANDING MAIN IDEAS For each of the following, write the letter of the best choice in the space provided.

_____ 1. Immigrants who wish to become citizens must do all of the following EXCEPT
  a. memorize the Constitution.
  b. fill out a petition for naturalization.
  c. appear before a naturalization official for questioning.
  d. take an oath of allegiance to the United States.

_____ 2. Many Germans settled in which state?
  a. MA
  b. SC
  c. NY
  d. PA

Main Idea Activities 1.3

We the People

VOCABULARY Some terms to understand:

- **population (p. 14):** number of people
- **decline (p. 14** decrease
- **rate (p. 14):** speed
- **projections (p. 15):** predictions
- **annexation (p. 15):** takeover
- **steady (p. 15):** even or constant
- **fluctuates (p. 16):** changes or rises and falls
- **relatively (p. 18):** comparatively

ORGANIZING INFORMATION Complete the following graphic organizer.

Factor	How Factor Has Changed with Time: Increase or Decrease?
Population	
Number of people living in rural areas	
Number of people living in suburbs	
Migration	
Diversity of population	
Size of household	
Age of population	

EVALUATING INFORMATION Mark each statement *T* if it is true or *F* if it is false.

_____ 1. The census not only tells us the size of each state's population but can also tell us about the people who live in the United States.

_____ 2. Nations grow in only one way—when the birthrate is greater than the death rate.

_____ 3. People believe that although the population itself will increase in the future, the rate of increase will drop.

Chapter 1, Main Idea Activities 1.3, continued

_____ **4.** In the past, many people moved from urban to rural areas.

_____ **5.** The majority of people in the United States live in metropolitan areas.

_____ **6.** Many people are moving from the Sunbelt to the Midwest and the Northeast.

_____ **7.** Hispanic Americans are the largest minority group in the United States.

_____ **8.** Many couples in the United States are having fewer children.

REVIEWING FACTS Choose the correct items from the following list to complete the statements below.

census	Sunbelt
birthrate	suburb
death rate	metropolitan area
rural area	migration

1. The _____ refers to the annual number of live births per 1,000 members of a population.

2. _____ involves the movement of large numbers of people from region to region.

3. The United States may conduct a _____ to see how many people live in a particular state.

4. _____ refers to the annual number of deaths per 1,000 members of a country's population.

5. If you live in an area surrounding a city, you live in a _____.

6. If you live in a region of farms, then you live in a _____.

7. The states in the South and West are known as the _____.

Name _____ Class _____ Date _____

Foundations of Government

VOCABULARY Some terms to understand:

- **enforces (p. 25):** insists on
- **ceremonial (p. 26):** formal or in name only
- **absolute (p. 26):** complete
- **consent (p. 26):** to agree
- **restricted (p. 29):** limited or controlled
- **violate (p. 29):** to break or go against
- **endangered (p. 29):** at risk

ORGANIZING INFORMATION Identify four purposes of government in our society, and write one in each of the boxes on the left. Then provide an example of how the government fulfills each purpose, and write one in each of the boxes on the right.

EVALUATING INFORMATION Mark each statement *T* if it is true or *F* if it is false.

_____ **1.** A government makes rules, but does not enforce them.

_____ **2.** Every country in the world has the same type of government.

_____ **3.** In most nations that have monarchs, the monarchs' power is greatly limited.

_____

Chapter 2, Main Idea Activities 2.1, continued

_____

_____ **4.** The two forms of democracy are direct and representative.

_____ **5.** The U.S. government provides its citizens with a system of money, trash collection, and highways.

REVIEWING FACTS Choose the correct terms from the following list to complete the statements below.

monarchies	democracy	laws
dictatorship	direct democracy	constitution
authoritarian	representative democracy	
totalitarian	republic	

1. The type of government in which the ruler has absolute control over the government

is a(n) _____.

2. In a(n) _____, the people elect representatives to carry on the work of government for them.

3. Countries controlled by kings or queens are _____.

4. Dictatorships are considered _____ when the ruler attempts to control all aspects of citizens' lives, including their religious, cultural, political, and even personal activities.

5. In general, a(n) _____ allows the people of the nation to either rule directly or elect officials who act on their behalf.

6. Dictatorships are _____, meaning that their rulers answer only to themselves, not to the people they rule.

7. In a(n) _____, all voters in a community meet in one place to make laws and decide what actions to take.

8. Rules of conduct for a group are called _____.

9. The United States is considered a(n) _____.

10. A(n) _____ is a written plan of government.

Name _____ Class _____ Date _____

Foundations of Government

VOCABULARY Some terms to understand:

- **philosophy (p. 31):** belief
- **will (p. 31):** to desire
- **legitimate (p. 31):** rightful or lawful
- **justify (p. 31):** to give reason for
- **entitled (p. 31):** allowed
- **association (p. 32):** connection
- **union (p. 32):** combination or a coming together
- **preferential (p. 33):** special or better
- **debt (p. 33):** owing money
- **disputes (p. 33):** arguments or disagreements
- **quarreled (p. 35):** fought

ORGANIZING INFORMATION Write in each box a weakness of the Articles of Confederation.

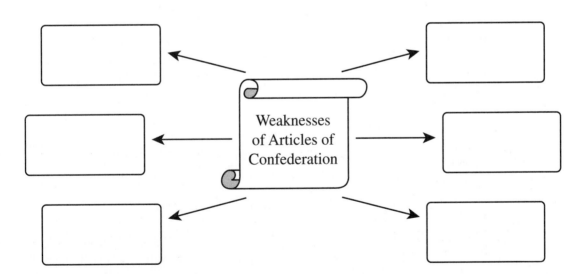

EVALUATING INFORMATION Mark each statement *T* if it is true or *F* if it is false.

_____ **1.** Before King George III began to enforce his policies, the colonies were for the most part self-supporting.

_____ **2.** The Declaration of Independence was approved by members of the Continental Congress on July 4, 1776.

Chapter 2, Main Idea Activities 2.2, continued

_____ **3.** Only some individuals have the right to life, liberty, and the pursuit of happiness, according to the Declaration of Independence.

_____ **4.** The Articles of Confederation were approved by only 10 states.

_____ **5.** The majority of people in the 13 states wanted a strong central government.

_____ **6.** The Articles of Confederation gave more power to the states and less to the national government.

_____ **7.** Under the Articles of Confederation, Congress had the power to force states to pay taxes.

_____ **8.** Among the problems the 13 states faced were disagreements over the location of boundary lines.

UNDERSTANDING MAIN IDEAS For each of the following, write the letter of the best choice in the space provided.

_____ **1.** A confederation is
   a. a firm union of states.
   b. the southern states.
   c. a loose association of states.
   d. the northern states.

_____ **2.** One goal of the Articles of Confederation was to give the _____ power.
   a. national government
   b. states
   c. king
   d. governors

_____ **3.** The term *sovereignty* means
   a. king or queen.
   b. absolute power.
   c. powerless.
   d. national power.

_____ **4.** Each of the following was a weakness of the government under the Articles of Confederation EXCEPT
   a. they gave the national government too much power.
   b. Congress lacked the power to collect taxes.
   c. the government could not control trade.
   d. Congress had trouble passing laws.

_____ **5.** The Declaration of Independence
   a. outlines the reasons the colonies wanted freedom from England.
   b. explains that the purpose of government is to protect human rights.
   c. a and b.
   d. none of the above.

CHAPTER 2

Main Idea Activities 2.3
Foundations of Government

VOCABULARY Some terms to understand:

- **endured (p. 40):** lasted
- **drafted (p. 40):** outlined
- **aided (p. 40):** helped
- **preside (p. 41):** to be in charge of, supervise, or head
- **diplomat (p. 41):** representative or public servant
- **framers (p. 43):** composers or writers
- **swamped (p. 45):** overwhelmed

REVIEWING FACTS Choose the correct terms from the following list to complete the statements below.

delegates	compromise	Federalists
bicameral	legislature	Antifederalists
federalism	ratification	
unitary system	Parliament	

1. The Constitution had to be sent to the states for _____, or approval.

2. Supporters of the Constitution who wanted a strong national government were called

_____.

3. A group of _____, or representatives, met in Independence Hall in Philadelphia.

4. _____ is the lawmaking body of Great Britain.

5. The delegates eventually had to _____ and each side gave up a part of its demands in order to reach a solution.

6. In a(n) _____, the national government possesses all legal power.

7. The Parliament is _____ because it consists of two parts, or houses.

Chapter 2, Main Idea Activities 2.3, continued

8. _____ divides a government's powers between the national government and state governments.

9. A serious disagreement over the representation in the lawmaking body, or

_____, arose.

10. People who opposed the new Constitution and did not want a strong national government were called _____.

EVALUATING INFORMATION Mark each statement *T* if it is true or *F* if it is false.

_____ **1.** Only two states, North Carolina and Rhode Island, did not approve the Constitution until after it went into effect.

_____ **2.** We no longer use the Constitution that was drafted in 1787.

_____ **3.** George Washington was chosen to preside over the Constitutional Convention.

_____ **4.** The Magna Carta allowed people to be put in prison and forced to leave the nation without a trial by a jury of peers.

_____ **5.** Parliament is bicameral.

_____ **6.** Constitutional Convention meetings were secret.

_____ **7.** George Washington kept a journal of what happened during each meeting of the Constitutional Convention.

_____ **8.** In a unitary system, the national government does not possess any legal power.

_____ **9.** Larger states wanted representation in the new national legislature to be based on the size of a state's population.

_____ **10.** In the Senate, states have equal representation, while in the House of Representatives, each state is represented according to the size of its population.

_____ **11.** By the time the Constitution was completed, every delegate was satisfied with every part of the document.

_____ **12.** When the states were deciding whether or not to ratify the Constitution, many people were swamped with pamphlets, letters to newspapers, and speeches representing both sides of the debate.

CHAPTER 3   Main Idea Activities 3.1

The U.S. Constitution

VOCABULARY Some terms to understand:

- **charter (p. 71):** agreement or contract
- **safeguard (p. 72):** protect or defend
- **dissatisfied (p. 73):** unhappy with
- **ensures (p. 73):** makes sure or guarantees
- **coin (p. 74):** create
- **exclusively (p. 75):** completely
- **affairs (p. 75):** dealings
- **charter (p. 75):** to hire or to employ
- **welfare (p. 75):** well-being or happiness
- **supreme (p. 75):** highest
- **restrictions (p. 75):** limits

ORGANIZING INFORMATION Complete the graphic organizer by comparing and contrasting the powers of the federal and state governments.

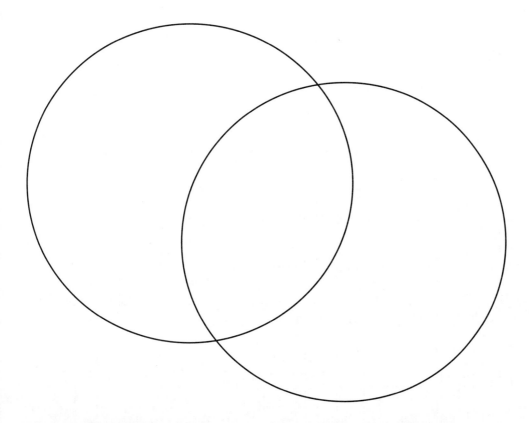

Powers of Federal Government   **Powers of State Government**

Chapter 3, Main Idea Activities 3.1, *continued*

EVALUATING INFORMATION Mark each statement *T* if it is true or *F* if it is false.

_____ **1.** The framers of the Constitution wanted to emphasize the importance of the people.

_____ **2.** The Preamble is law.

_____ **3.** If U.S. citizens become dissatisfied with the way their representatives are governing, there is nothing they can do.

_____ **4.** Our republic is based upon the idea of minority rule.

_____ **5.** Under federalism the powers of government are divided between the national government and the state government.

_____ **6.** The U.S. system of government is based in part on the Magna Carta.

REVIEWING FACTS Choose the correct terms from the following list to complete the statements below.

popular sovereignty   concurrent powers
majority rule   limited government
delegated powers   Preamble
reserved powers

1. Our government is a _____, meaning that there are certain limitations to its power.

2. The powers that are set aside for the states or the people are called

_____.

3. The powers that the Constitution specifically gives to the federal government are

called _____.

4. _____ means the consent of the governed.

5. The opening sentence of the Constitution is the _____; it explains why the U.S. Constitution was written.

6. The United States adheres to _____ so that when people disagree, everyone accepts the decision of the majority.

7. Powers shared by both the federal and state governments are called

_____.

CHAPTER **3**   Main Idea Activities 3.2

The U.S. Constitution

VOCABULARY Some terms to understand:

• **provisions (p. 77):** conditions, terms, or rules

• **distributes (p. 77):** spreads out

• **enforce (p. 78):** apply or put into action

• **assume (p. 79):** take on

• **overriding (p. 79):** cancelling or stopping something after it has been approved

ORGANIZING INFORMATION Complete the graphic organizer below by filling in the names of the three branches of government. Also, briefly summarize the powers of each branch.

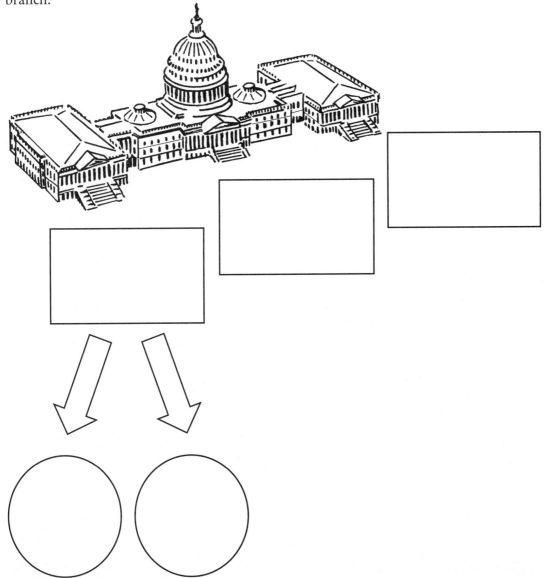

Chapter 3, Main Idea Activities 3.2, continued

EVALUATING INFORMATION Mark each statement *T* if it is true or *F* if it is false.

_____ **1.** The executive branch is made up of two houses—the Senate and the House of Representatives.

_____ **2.** The judicial branch has the most power of all three branches.

_____ **3.** The president has the power to veto proposed laws.

_____ **4.** The executive branch includes the president and vice president.

_____ **5.** The Supreme Court is the head of the judicial branch.

UNDERSTANDING MAIN IDEAS For each of the following, write the letter of the best choice in the space provided.

_____ **1.** All of the following are branches of the U.S. government EXCEPT
    a. executive.
    b. Senate.
    c. judicial.
    d. legislative.

_____ **2.** Another name for the legislative branch is
    a. Congress.
    b. Senate.
    c. House of Representatives.
    d. president.

_____ **3.** The name given to the system that makes sure no branch becomes too powerful is
    a. equal powers.
    b. checks and balances.
    c. democracy.
    d. none of the above.

_____ **4.** The judicial branch
    a. makes laws.
    b. carries out laws.
    c. interprets laws.
    d. holds the most power.

_____ **5.** Original provisions in the Constitution state that which of the following holds the most power?
    a. president
    b. Congress
    c. Supreme Court
    d. none of the above

_____ **6.** The president heads
    a. the legislative branch.
    b. the executive branch.
    c. the judicial branch.
    d. all of the branches.

CHAPTER 3   Main Idea Activities 3.3

The U.S. Constitution

VOCABULARY Some terms to understand:

• **flexibility (p. 82):** changes easily

• **foresee (p. 82):** predict

• **convention (p. 83):** an assembly or gathering of people

• **clause (p. 84):** a section

• **wages (p. 84):** salaries

• **seldom (p. 84):** hardly ever

ORGANIZING INFORMATION Complete the graphic organizer below by filling in each of the steps necessary to amend the Constitution. Also fill in the two ways that each step may be completed.

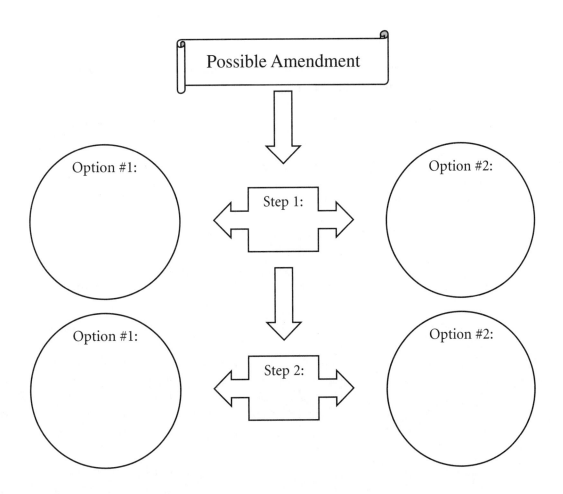

Chapter 3, Main Idea Activities 3.3, continued

EVALUATING INFORMATION Mark each statement *T* if it is true or *F* if it is false.

_____ **1.** Unfortunately, the Constitution is not very flexible.

_____ **2.** Amendment is one of the ways the Constitution and the government can respond to the changing needs of the country.

_____ **3.** An amendment is a written change made to the Constitution.

_____ **4.** Only the president needs to approve an amendment for it to be written into the Constitution.

_____ **5.** Two thirds of the states can ask Congress to call a national convention to propose an amendment; however, this method has never been used successfully.

_____ **6.** The word ratify means to reject.

_____ **7.** Most of the amendments that have been approved have been sent to the state legislatures for approval.

_____ **8.** An amendment cannot be canceled if the people decide they do not like the effect it is having on the country.

_____ **9.** Many traditions observed by the government are part of an unwritten Constitution.

_____ **10.** The president meets regularly with his cabinet.

_____ **11.** The U.S. Constitution can be considered a "living document."

_____ **12.** The framers of the Constitution believed that they could foresee all of the changes the United States would undergo.

Main Idea Activities 4.1

Rights and Responsibilities

VOCABULARY Some terms to understand:

- **ratification (p. 89):** approval
- **amendments (p. 89):** improvements or corrections
- **totalitarian (p. 90):** a form of government in which one person or group of people has complete control
- **absolute (p. 90):** complete or without limits
- **dictates (p. 90):** orders or commands
- **falsehoods (p. 91):** statements that are untrue
- **arms (p. 92):** weapons
- **regulated (p. 92):** controlled
- **seizure (p. 93):** the act of taking something by force
- **hasty (p. 93):** quick, swift, or fast
- **prompt (p. 94):** on time

CLASSIFYING INFORMATION Write the name of the amendment below the picture of the object it protects.

_____   _____

_____   _____

Chapter 4, Main Idea Activities 4.1, continued

EVALUATING INFORMATION Mark each statement *T* if it is true or *F* if it is false.

_____ **1.** Ten years after the new U.S. government went into effect, the Bill of Rights was added.

_____ **2.** The First Amendment allows Americans to practice any religion they wish.

_____ **3.** Although the First Amendment guarantees freedom of speech, Americans cannot criticize the government.

_____ **4.** Freedom of the press allows Americans the right to express their thoughts freely in writing. However they must not make false statements that ruin a person's reputation.

_____ **5.** A petition is a formal request that usually asks a group in power to do something or stop doing something.

_____ **6.** The Second Amendment protects the right to bear arms.

_____ **7.** According to the Fourth Amendment, a search can only be conducted if a judge has issued a search warrant.

_____ **8.** Double jeopardy means that a person may be tried a second time for the same crime.

REVIEWING FACTS Choose the correct items from the following list to complete the statements below.

separation of church and state	indicted	search warrant
libel	slander	eminent domain

1. Courts have decided to prevent people from saying prayers in public schools because

of the _____.

2. A(n) _____ can only be issued if there is good reason to believe that evidence about a crime will be found.

3. The government's power to take citizens' property for public use is known as

_____.

4. If a person knowingly makes false statements that hurt another person's reputation,

the person has committed _____.

5. If a journalist writes statements that are untrue and hurt another person's reputation,

he or she may be sued for _____.

6. If a person is _____, he or she is formally accused of a crime.

CHAPTER **4**

Main Idea Activities 4.2

Rights and Responsibilities

VOCABULARY Some terms to understand:

• **expanded (p. 96):** increased

• **foundation (p. 96):** starting point or source

• **liberty (p. 97):** freedom

• **eligible (p. 97):** qualified

• **second-class (p. 98):** second best or not as good as others

ORGANIZING INFORMATION Fill in the chart below with the appropriate information.

Amendment	What the Amendment Did
Thirteenth	1.
Fourteenth	2.
3.	Granted African Americans the right to vote
4.	Voters could elect their states' senators
Nineteenth	5.
Twenty-third	6.
7.	Forbade the poll tax
Twenty-sixth	8.

EVALUATING INFORMATION Mark each statement *T* if it is true or *F* if it is false.

_____ **1.** The Thirteenth Amendment not only outlawed slavery but it also gave African Americans the right to vote.

_____ **2.** Suffrage refers to the right to vote for women only.

_____ **3.** Women such as Susan B. Anthony and Elizabeth Cady Stanton helped women gain the right to vote.

_____ **4.** Before the ratification of the Twenty-third Amendment, people living in Washington, D.C., could not vote in national elections.

_____ **5.** Many people believed that the poll tax was meant to prevent poor people from voting.

_____ **6.** The Twenty-sixth Amendment increased the voting age from 18 to 21.

_____ **7.** Today the Constitution has a total of 27 amendments.

Chapter 4, Main Idea Activities 4.2, continued

UNDERSTANDING MAIN IDEAS For each of the following, write the letter of the best choice in the space provided.

_____ **1.** The Emancipation Proclamation
   a. freed all slaves.
   b. gave African Americans the right to vote.
   c. freed only some slaves.
   d. gave women the right to vote.

_____ **2.** When the Constitution was first written, it
   a. did not mention voting rights.
   b. allowed all men to vote.
   c. forbade women from voting.
   d. allowed all people, regardless of race or sex, to vote.

_____ **3.** The first state to give women the right to vote was
   a. Massachusetts
   b. California
   c. Wyoming
   d. Utah

_____ **4.** The Fifteenth Amendment
   a. gave African Americans the right to vote.
   b. gave women the right to vote.
   c. gave African Americans citizenship.
   d. gave women citizenship.

_____ **5.** Today the Constitution has a total of
   a. 1000 amendments.
   b. 2 amendments.
   c. 27 amendments.
   d. 0 amendments.

_____ **6.** The Thirteenth Amendment was ratified in
   a. 1950.
   b. 1865.
   c. 1665.
   d. 1700.

_____ **7.** Before amendments regarding voting were added to the Constitution,
   a. only males over 21 who owned property could vote.
   b. everyone could vote.
   c. men and women could vote.
   d. only those over 18 could vote.

_____ **8.** The following helped women gain the right to vote EXCEPT
   a. Martha Washington.
   b. Elizabeth Cady Stanton.
   c. Susan B. Anthony.
   d. Carrie Chapman Catt.

Name _____ Class _____ Date _____

Rights and Responsibilities

VOCABULARY Some terms to understand:

- **duty (p. 100):** responsibility or job you are expected to do
- **ignorance (p. 100):** lack of knowledge
- **fulfill (p. 101):** to complete or finish
- **maintaining (p. 101):** keeping or protecting
- **implemented (p. 102):** put into operation
- **inconvenient (p. 102):** not happening at a preferable time
- **ideal (p. 103):** the best or a model
- **consent (p. 103):** permission or approval
- **policies (p. 103):** rules

CLASSIFYING INFORMATION Fill in the blanks beneath the pictures with the following phrases.

obeying the law   attending school
paying taxes   serving in the armed forces
appearing in court

Duties of Citizenship

_____

_____

_____

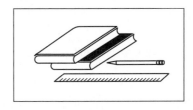

_____

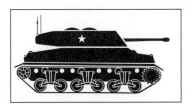

_____

Chapter 4, Main Idea Activities 4.3, continued

EVALUATING INFORMATION Mark each statement *T* if it is true or *F* if it is false.

_____ **1.** You can find the duties of all citizens described in the Constitution and in the laws of the nation and the states.

_____ **2.** Public schools guarantee only some young people the opportunity to be educated.

_____ **3.** Taxes pay for salaries in the police force, fire department, and armed forces.

_____ **4.** At age 21, all men must register for the draft.

_____ **5.** Men have always been required to register for the draft.

_____ **6.** As an American citizen, if you are called to be a member of a jury, you may say no.

_____ **7.** American citizens are not required by law to vote.

_____ **8.** Before voting, you should learn what policies are favored by each candidate running for office.

_____ **9.** Each citizen is required to serve as a government official.

_____ **10.** Volunteering in your community is not a duty, but a responsibility.

REVIEWING FACTS Choose the correct items from the following list to complete the statements below.

duties   taxes   draft

1. _____ pay for many services provided by the government, such as police and fire protection.

2. A _____ requires each 18-year-old male to register to serve in the armed forces.

3. Actions that citizens must perform are _____.

Main Idea Activities 5.1

The Legislative Branch

VOCABULARY Some terms to understand:

- **haste (p. 113):** speed
- **distributed (p. 114):** spread out or divided
- **entitled (p. 114):** allowed or given the right
- **boundaries (p. 114):** borders
- **favor (p. 114):** prefer or support
- **resigns (p. 114):** quits
- **vacancy (p. 114):** available job
- **prior (p. 115):** earlier or previous
- **infringe (p. 115):** break or violate
- **qualifications (p. 116):** experiences
- **controversial (p. 117):** producing conflict
- **disclosure (p. 118):** revealing
- **grounds (p. 118):** reasons

ORGANIZING INFORMATION Complete the chart below to compare the House of Representatives and the Senate.

	House of Representatives	Senate
Number of members		
Length of term		
Qualifications		

Chapter 5, Main Idea Activities 5.1, continued

EVALUATING INFORMATION Mark each statement *T* if it is true or *F* if it is false.

_____ **1.** Both the House of Representatives and the Senate make laws.

_____ **2.** One reason that the leaders who drew up the Constitution created a bicameral legislature was to give some states more power than others.

_____ **3.** Congress decides how the seats are distributed in the House of Representatives according to each state's population.

_____ **4.** Sometimes state legislators draw distinct lines for congressional districts that favor a particular political party, resulting in oddly shaped districts.

_____ **5.** If a representative cannot serve the entire term, the government must function with this vacancy.

_____ **6.** The first Senate consisted of 26 senators.

_____ **7.** Many members of Congress have had little if any experience in politics before being elected.

_____ **8.** Members of Congress can be arrested during a meeting in Congress.

REVIEWING FACTS Choose the correct terms from the following list to complete the statements below.

apportioned   franking privilege   censure
gerrymandering   immunity
term limits   expulsion

1. Members of Congress have the _____, or right to mail official letters or packages free of charge.

2. Serious misconduct by a member of Congress may end in that person's

_____ from office.

3. Congress determines how the seats in the House are to be

_____ every 10 years after the census is taken.

4. Members of Congress have _____, or legal protection.

5. When state legislators draw distinct district lines that favor a particular political

party, it is called _____.

CHAPTER (5)   Main Idea Activities 5.2

The Legislative Branch

VOCABULARY Some terms to understand:

- **adjourned (p. 119):** stopped
- **presiding (p. 120):** in charge of
- **persuade (p. 121):** to convince
- **conduct (p. 121):** to do or perform
- **permanent (p. 122):** lasting
- **hearings (p. 122):** trials or investigations
- **scandals (p. 122):** disgraces or dishonors
- **disbanded (p. 122):** broke up
- **enables (p. 123):** allows or helps
- **specialize (p. 123):** to focus on

ORGANIZING INFORMATION The rectangles below represent the House of Representatives and the Senate. The circles within the rectangles represent the representatives and senators. Label the circles with the appropriate titles, given below, based upon where they are in the "room."

House of Representatives

    majority leader
    minority leader
    Speaker of the House
    majority party
    minority party

Senate

    vice president (if absent)
    president *pro tempore*
    majority leader
    minority leader
    majority party
    minority party

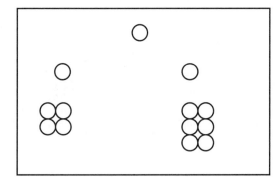

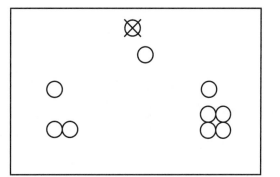

Chapter 5, Main Idea Activities 5.2, continued

EVALUATING INFORMATION Mark each statement *T* if it is true or *F* if it is false.

_____ **1.** If serious problems arise after Congress has adjourned its regular session, the president may call Congress to meet in a special session.

_____ **2.** Caucuses occur when Republican and Democratic members in each house gather separately in private meetings.

_____ **3.** The political party with the least members in each house is called the majority party.

_____ **4.** The vice president is the presiding officer of the Senate, and therefore can participate in Senate debates.

_____ **5.** Each member of the House usually serves on three to five major standing committees.

_____ **6.** Usually a committee chairperson is the majority party member with the most years of service on the committee.

UNDERSTANDING MAIN IDEAS For each of the following, write the letter of the best choice in the space provided.

_____ **1.** A committee made up of an equal number of representatives and senators is called a
   a. select committee.
   b. standing committee.
   c. joint committee.
   d. subcommittee.

_____ **2.** The job of a party whip is to
   a. persuade members to vote a certain way.
   b. preside over his or her party.
   c. preside over the House and Senate.
   d. take over for the vice president if he or she is absent.

_____ **3.** In each term of Congress there are how many regular sessions?
   a. one
   b. two
   c. three
   d. four

_____ **4.** The most powerful officers of the Senate are
   a. the party whips.
   b. the majority leader.
   c. the minority leader.
   d. b and c.

CHAPTER **5** Main Idea Activities 5.3

The Legislative Branch

VOCABULARY Some terms to understand:

- **debts (p. 126):** amount not paid
- **welfare (p. 126):** well-being
- **regulate (p. 127):** to control
- **dismissed (p. 128):** sent away
- **resign (p. 129):** to give up one's position
- **exceeds (p. 130):** goes beyond
- **essential (p. 131):** necessary or important, fundamental or key

REVIEWING FACTS Choose the correct terms from the following list to complete the statements below.

elastic clause	impeached	writ of *habeas corpus*
implied powers	*ex post facto* law	constituents
treason	bill of attainder	

1. A(n) _____ requires that a person accused of a crime be brought to court.

2. The _____ states that Congress has the power "to make all laws which shall be necessary and proper for carrying into execution the foregoing powers."

3. Bill Clinton was _____ on charges that he lied under oath and obstructed justice.

4. The powers that Congress claims under the elastic clauses are called

_____.

5. A law that sentences a person to prison without a trial is called a(n)

_____.

6. The people who live in a congressmember's home district or state are referred to as

_____.

7. An act that betrays or endangers one's country is called _____.

8. A law that applies to an action that took place before the law was passed is called a(n)

_____.

Name _____ Class _____ Date _____

EVALUATING INFORMATION Mark each statement *T* if it is true or *F* if it is false.

_____ **1.** Only in special circumstances can a person go to prison without a trial.

_____ **2.** A tax on exports allows the government to increase its foreign and domestic trade.

_____ **3.** Congress can raise and collect taxes, borrow money, and print and coin money.

_____ **4.** To ensure that laws are upheld, Congress has established a system of national courts.

_____ **5.** The Constitution specifically gives Congress the power to set up national military academies.

_____ **6.** Only three presidents have ever been impeached.

_____ **7.** The vice president acts as the judge during an impeachment hearing, even if the president is impeached.

_____ **8.** The House of Representatives may choose the president if no presidential candidate receives the number of electoral votes needed to be elected.

_____ **9.** The powers of Congress are not limited.

_____ **10.** Congress cannot pass laws giving a state or group of states an unfair trade advantage.

_____ **11.** Congress may set a uniform standard of weights and measures.

_____ **12.** Congress does not have the power to declare war.

_____ **13.** All treaties with foreign nations must be approved in the Senate by a two-thirds vote.

_____ **14.** All impeachment trials are held in the House of Representatives.

CHAPTER **5**

Main Idea Activities 5.4

The Legislative Branch

VOCABULARY Some terms to understand:

- **exception (p. 132):** rule does not apply in this instance
- **proceedings (p. 134):** events
- **testify (p. 135):** to be a witness
- **debate (p. 136):** to argue or discuss
- **revises (p. 137):** changes
- **hasty (p. 139):** quick

ORGANIZING INFORMATION Put the following steps in the flow chart in the correct order to show how a bill becomes a law.

Bill is written out.
Senate passes bill.
Congressmembers have idea for bill.
Bill is sent to standing committee.

President approves the bill.
Bill is printed in *Congressional Record*.
House passes bill.
Bill is revised.

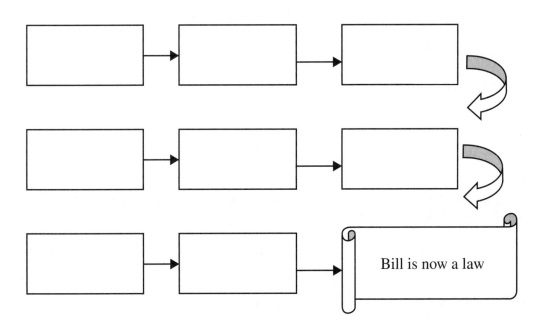

Bill is now a law

Chapter 5, Main Idea Activities 5.4, continued

EVALUATING INFORMATION Mark each statement *T* if it is true or *F* if it is false.

_____ **1.** Only members of Congress can create ideas for a bill.

_____ **2.** Only members of Congress can introduce a bill.

_____ **3.** Both Congress and the House of Representatives can revise the bill.

_____ **4.** After a bill is introduced, it is sent to a standing committee for study.

_____ **5.** Letters from citizens have no effect on whether a bill is passed.

_____ **6.** If the president keeps the bill for 10 days without signing it, and Congress is in session, the bill can become a law without the president's signature.

_____ **7.** The process through which a bill becomes a law is extremely short.

_____ **8.** Proposed bills must be written out.

REVIEWING FACTS Choose the correct terms from the following list to complete the statements below.

appropriation bill	roll-call vote	pocket veto
act	filibuster	
quorum	cloture	

1. The method of delay in which senators talk for many hours about a bill is called a(n)

_____.

2. _____ is a bill approving the spending of money.

3. A(n) _____, or majority of members, must be present either during the Committee of the Whole or when the House meets in a formal session in order to do business.

4. A(n) _____ occurs when the names of each member of the House is called and a record is made of his or her vote.

5. Limit on debate in the Senate is called _____.

CHAPTER **6**

Main Idea Activities 6.1

The Executive Branch

VOCABULARY Some terms to understand:

- **tendencies (p. 143):** trends
- **precedent (p. 144):** an example or guide
- **restriction (p. 144):** limit
- **insignificant (p. 145):** not important
- **succession (p. 146):** sequence or series

ORGANIZING INFORMATION Fill in the title of the person below the picture, indicating the levels of presidential succession.

vice president
_____

_____

_____

_____

EVALUATING INFORMATION Mark each statement *T* if it is true or *F* if it is false.

_____ **1.** There have been 42 presidents.

_____ **2.** To be elected president, one does not necessarily need to be a native-born U.S. citizen.

_____ **3.** One must be a resident of the United States for at least 14 years to be president.

_____ **4.** Today, a president can serve a maximum of three terms.

_____ **5.** John Adams said that the office of vice president was "the most significant" office ever invented.

_____ **6.** The vice president serves a four-year term.

Chapter 6, Main Idea Activities 6.1, continued

_____ **7.** The Twenty-fifth Amendment states that if a president dies or resigns, a new vice president must be approved by a majority vote of both houses of Congress.

_____ **8.** If the president is ill and cannot complete his or her duties, the vice president serves in his or her place until he or she is well again.

_____ **9.** To be president, one must be at least 25 years of age.

_____ **10.** So far, only Protestants have served as president.

_____ **11.** Because the president is able to live in the White House, he or she does not have a regular salary.

_____ **12.** In recent years, presidents have given their vice presidents more responsibilities.

REVIEWING FACTS Choose the correct terms from the following list to complete the statements below.

men	presidential succession
one	Camp David
two	Speaker of the House

1. The order in which the office of president is to be filled is called

_____.

2. George Washington served _____ term(s).

3. The president may vacation at _____.

4. So far, all presidents have been _____.

5. If the vice president is unable to serve as president, the _____ serves as president.

CHAPTER 6 Main Idea Activities 6.2

The Executive Branch

VOCABULARY Some terms to understand:

- **phases (p. 147):** stages
- **pressing (p. 147):** urgent
- **recall (p. 148):** to recollect or remember
- **ensure (p. 149):** to make certain or guarantee
- **secure (p. 149):** maintain
- **tact (p. 149):** skill in dealing with others
- **promote (p. 150):** encourage or support
- **corresponds (p. 150):** communicates or keeps in touch
- **consent (p. 150):** to give permission or approval

EVALUATING INFORMATION Mark each statement *T* if it is true or *F* if it is false.

_____ **1.** The Constitution requires that the president make suggestions to Congress.

_____ **2.** The president allows Congress to deal completely with economic concerns; he or she does not make suggestions.

_____ **3.** The president may declare war.

_____ **4.** The president serves as commander in chief of the armed forces.

_____ **5.** The president assigns people the responsibility of making treaties with other countries.

_____ **6.** The Constitution gives the president the power to appoint Supreme Court justices and other federal judges.

_____ **7.** The president serves as chief of state and political party leader.

_____ **8.** President John F. Kennedy established the custom of reporting directly to the American people through weekly radio addresses.

_____ **9.** The president does not usually deal with foreign countries.

_____ **10.** The president is often called the nation's chief executive.

Chapter 6, Main Idea Activities 6.2, continued

REVIEWING FACTS Choose the correct items from the following list to complete the statements below.

foreign policy   diplomatic notes   commutation
treaties   reprieve
diplomacy   pardon

1. Written communications with leaders of foreign governments are called

_____.

2. The president may grant a _____, freeing a person convicted of a crime from serving out the sentence.

3. The president makes _____, or written agreements, with other countries.

4. The government's plan for interacting with other countries of the world is called

_____.

5. A _____ postpones the carrying out of a person's sentence.

UNDERSTANDING MAIN IDEAS For each of the following, write the letter of the best choice in the space provided.

_____ 1. In the State of the Union address to Congress, the president makes recommendations involving
   a. foreign policy.
   b. economics.
   c. legislation.
   d. all of the above.

_____ 2. The president also holds the title of
   a. commander in chief.
   b. vice president.
   c. Speaker of the House.
   d. none of the above.

_____ 3. The president does all of the following regarding foreign policy EXCEPT
   a. making treaties with other nations.
   b. appointing officials to represent the United States in other countries.
   c. enforcing laws of the United States on foreign countries.
   d. securing friendly relations with foreign governments.

CHAPTER **6**   Main Idea Activities 6.3

The Executive Branch

VOCABULARY Some terms to understand:

- **significantly (p. 153):** drastically

- **domestic (p. 153):** national

- **promote (p. 153):** to support

- **designate (p. 154):** to assign

- **eliminate (p. 154):** to get rid of

- **adapt (p. 154):** to get used to or adjust

- **corporate (p. 156):** having to do with a business or company

- **goods (p. 156):** supplies

- **equipping (p. 157):** providing

REVIEWING FACTS Choose the correct terms from the following list to complete the statements below.

budget	ambassadors	civilian
executive departments	embassy	passports
secretary	ministers	visas
attorney general	consul	counterfeiting

1. The official residence and offices of an ambassador in a foreign country is called a(n)

_____.

2. A(n) _____ represents U.S. commercial interests in foreign countries.

3. A(n) _____ is a plan of income and spending.

4. The head of the Department of Justice is called the _____.

5. As of 2003, there were 15 _____ in the federal government which had specific areas of responsibility.

6. The title of most cabinet members is _____.

7. The Secret Service helps to prevent _____, or the making and distributing of fake money.

8. _____ are the highest-ranking U.S. representatives in foreign countries.

Chapter 6, Main Idea Activities 6.3, continued

9. In a few smaller countries, _____ are ranked below ambassadors and represent the United States.

10. _____ allow foreigners to come to the United States.

11. _____ are formal documents that allow U.S. citizens to travel abroad.

12. A nonmilitary person, or _____, heads the Department of Defense.

EVALUATING INFORMATION Mark each statement *T* if it is true or *F* if it is false.

_____ **1.** The National Security Council is the president's top-ranking group of advisers on all matters concerning defense and security.

_____ **2.** The leaders who wrote the Constitution tried to work out every detail of government.

_____ **3.** The cabinet consists of the heads of the 15 executive departments and any other officials the president chooses.

_____ **4.** The Senate does not have to approve members of the cabinet.

_____ **5.** The Department of State deals with foreign policy.

_____ **6.** The Department of the Interior enforces federal laws.

_____ **7.** The Department of Agriculture helps farmers raise and market crops.

_____ **8.** The Bureau of Labor Statistics is a division of the Department of Agriculture.

_____ **9.** The federal government helps city and state governments provide public housing.

_____ **10.** The Department of Veterans Affairs is responsible for administering government benefits to U.S. veterans and their families.

The Executive Branch

VOCABULARY Some terms to understand:

- **specialized (p. 163):** expert or focused on something
- **function (p. 163):** work
- **independent (p. 163):** responsible for oneself
- **discrimination (p. 163):** prejudice or inequality
- **assist (p. 163):** to help
- **violators (p. 164):** those who break the law
- **remedy (p. 164):** to fix or cure
- **interfere (p. 164):** get in the way of

ORGANIZING INFORMATION Fill in the chart to compare independent agencies, regulatory commissions, and the federal bureaucracy.

	Independent Agencies	Regulatory Commissions	Federal Bureaucracy
Purpose			
Examples and what they do			

EVALUATING INFORMATION Mark each statement *T* if it is true or *F* if it is false.

_____ **1.** Some independent agencies serve all executive departments.

_____ **2.** There are about 10 independent agencies.

_____ **3.** The National Aeronautics and Space Administration (NASA) is an example of an independent agency.

_____ **4.** Regulatory commissions' decisions often have the force of law.

_____ **5.** The Federal Election Commission cuts public funding of presidential elections.

_____ **6.** Some people believe the regulatory commissions interfere too much in their lives.

Chapter 6, Main Idea Activities 6.4, *continued*

_____ **7.** Almost 3 million people work in the federal bureaucracy.

_____ **8.** In order to be a part of the federal bureaucracy, one must live in Washington, D.C.

_____ **9.** Some lawyers and scientists are part of the federal bureaucracy.

_____ **10.** The bureaucracy has few rules and regulations so that things are carried out quickly.

_____ **11.** Regulatory commissions are a form of independent agency.

_____ **12.** The Farm Credit Administration is a regulatory commission.

REVIEWING FACTS Choose the correct terms from the following list to complete the statements below.

independent agency	Office of Personnel Management
regulatory commission	Consumer Product Safety Commission
bureaucracy	National Labor Relations Board

1. The _____ would deal with such problems as a toy that could cause a child to choke.

2. The decisions of a(n) _____ often have the force of law.

3. The _____ helps prevent unfair labor practices among businesses.

4. Each _____ was created by Congress to perform a specific job.

5. The _____ gives tests to people who want to apply for jobs with the federal government.

CHAPTER **7**   Main Idea Activities 7.1

The Judicial Branch

VOCABULARY Some terms to understand:

- **predictable (p. 169):** expected
- **position (p. 169):** feelings or belief
- **supreme (p. 170):** highest
- **regulating (p. 170):** controlling
- **recklessly (p. 170):** without care or thought
- **just (p. 172):** fair
- **innocent (p. 171):** blameless or guiltless
- **administer (p. 171):** to direct or control
- **appoint (p. 172):** to hire
- **justify (p. 172):** give a reason for
- **accurate (p. 173):** exact or correct

ORGANIZING INFORMATION Provide a definition and example of each type of law.

	Statutory Law	Common Law	Administrative Law	Constitutional Law
Definition				
Example				

EVALUATING INFORMATION Mark each statement *T* if it is true or *F* if it is false.

_____ **1.** No matter how serious the crime, any accused person must be given a fair public trial.

_____ **2.** U.S. law assumes that a person is guilty until proven innocent.

_____ **3.** Every American has the right to a fair public trial.

_____ **4.** An accused person may have a lawyer only if he or she can afford it.

_____ **5.** All accused persons may be released from jail on bail.

_____ **6.** If a person is arrested on suspicion of a crime, he or she will certainly go to trial.

Chapter 7, Main Idea Activities 7.1, continued

_____ **7.** The Sixth Amendment to the Constitution guarantees an accused person the right to be tried before a trial jury.

_____ **8.** Usually the jury's verdict must be a unanimous vote.

_____ **9.** If the jury cannot reach a verdict, then the accused person is automatically set free.

_____ **10.** It is possible that a person could appeal his or her case to the Supreme Court.

REVIEWING FACTS Choose the correct terms from the following list to complete the statements below.

cross-examine	testimony	jurors
precedent	appeal	verdict
common law	petit jury	hung jury

1. To ensure that cases are decided fairly, the U.S. court system provides the right to

_____, or ask for a review of the case.

2. If a jury cannot reach a verdict, it is called a(n) _____.

3. Many judges might follow a(n) _____, or earlier decision, when considering a case.

4. Lawyers must question witnesses to ensure that _____, or evidence given in court, is accurate.

5. Another name for a trial jury is a(n) _____.

6. _____ are those people who sit on the jury.

7. Customary, or _____ law, comes from judges' decisions.

8. A decision reached by a jury is called a(n) _____.

9. Lawyers may question, or _____, witnesses.

The Judicial Branch

VOCABULARY Some terms to understand:

- **interpret (p. 174):** to read and determine what something means
- **violating (p. 174):** breaking the rules
- **authority (p. 175):** power
- **provision (p. 176):** condition or terms
- **convenient (p. 176):** handy or well-located
- **minor (p. 176):** small or unimportant
- **panel (p. 177):** group
- **chiefly (p. 178):** mainly or mostly
- **imports (p. 179):** goods brought into the United States

REVIEWING FACTS Choose the correct terms from the following list to complete the statements below.

jurisdiction	district courts	circuit
courts of appeals	marshal	court-martial
original jurisdiction	subpoena	territorial courts

1. People in the armed services who are accused of breaking a military law are tried at

a(n) _____ conducted by military officers.

2. One job that a(n) _____ does is to deliver official court orders.

3. The lowest courts are trial courts, and therefore, have _____ jurisdiction, or the authority to be the first courts in which most federal cases are heard.

4. The 12 U.S. courts of appeals cover a large judicial district known as a(n)

_____ .

5. _____ is defined as the authority to interpret and administer the law.

6. _____ were established by Congress to administer justice to the people living in U.S. territorial possessions.

7. A(n) _____ is an official court order requiring persons to appear in court.

8. The _____ review cases that are appealed from district courts.

Chapter 7, Main Idea Activities 7.2, continued

EVALUATING INFORMATION Mark each statement *T* if it is true or *F* if it is false.

_____ **1.** Anyone accused of disobeying any part of the U.S. Constitution may be brought to trial in a federal court.

_____ **2.** Appellate jurisdiction has authority over original jurisdiction.

_____ **3.** There is at least one district court in each of the 50 states and in the District of Columbia.

_____ **4.** U.S. marshals cannot arrest people accused of breaking federal laws.

_____ **5.** Jury trials take place in the courts of appeals.

_____ **6.** The U.S. Supreme Court is the highest court in the land.

_____ **7.** The Court of Federal Claims hears cases involving money claims against the federal government.

_____ **8.** All federal courts are presided over by judges approved by the president and the Senate.

UNDERSTANDING MAIN IDEAS For each of the following, write the letter of the best choice in the space provided.

_____ **1.** All of the following can be brought to trial in federal courts EXCEPT
    a. crimes committed on certain types of federal property.
    b. lawsuits between citizens of different states.
    c. crimes committed on U.S. ships at sea.
    d. appeals brought by military veterans against the Department of Veterans Affairs.

_____ **2.** The 50 states are divided into _____ circuits.
    a. 10
    b. 11
    c. 25
    d. 50

_____ **3.** All of the following are district court officials EXCEPT
    a. U.S. attorneys.
    b. military personnel.
    c. magistrate judges.
    d. marshals.

_____ **4.** Other federal courts include the
    a. U.S. Tax Court.
    b. Court of Automobiles.
    c. U.S. Court of Transportation.
    d. Court of Justice.

CHAPTER **7**

Main Idea Activities 7.3

The Judicial Branch

VOCABULARY Some terms to understand:

- **forcibly (p. 182):** by force
- **ultimate (p. 183):** final or highest
- **promoted (p. 183):** supported
- **significant (p. 184):** important or major
- **adjourns (p. 185):** stops
- **binding (p. 185):** required
- **uphold (p. 185):** to support or defend
- **unanimous (p. 187):** agreed upon by all
- **deliberate (p. 187):** on purpose or planned
- **ensure (p. 188):** to make certain
- **eliminate (p. 188):** to get rid of
- **controversy (p. 189):** disagreement or argument
- **outcry (p. 189):** protest or disagreement

ORGANIZING INFORMATION Number the boxes below to illustrate the order the Supreme Court hears a case.

_____ Justice writes the opinion of the court.	_____ Lawyers for each side present oral arguments.	_____ Justices agree to hear a particular case.

_____ Justices study briefs prepared by lawyers.	_____ Justices question lawyers.

Chapter 7, Main Idea Activities 7.3, continued

EVALUATING INFORMATION Mark each statement *T* if it is true or *F* if it is false.

_____ **1.** The number of justices of the Supreme Court has been set at nine since 1869.

_____ **2.** The Constitution requires that a Supreme Court justice be a lawyer.

_____ **3.** The Constitution does not specifically give the judicial branch the power of judicial review.

_____ **4.** John Marshall established that the Supreme Court has the power to reverse the decisions of state courts.

_____ **5.** The Supreme Court reviews all cases that appeal to it.

_____ **6.** If the Supreme Court refuses to review a case, the decision of the lower court is reversed.

_____ **7.** A justice may agree with the decision of the majority but for different reasons.

_____ **8.** The Supreme Court can rule that a law passed by Congress is unconstitutional.

_____ **9.** The case *Plessy* v. *Ferguson* desegregated schools.

_____ **10.** By law, police must inform arrested suspects that if they cannot afford a lawyer, one will be given to them.

_____ **11.** President Franklin D. Roosevelt officially added more justices to the Supreme Court.

_____ **12.** There are no limits on the Supreme Court's power.

_____ **13.** Justices are appointed to the Supreme Court for 10-year terms.

_____ **14.** The Supreme Court hears about 1,000 cases each year.

VOCABULARY Some terms to understand:

• **conducting (p. 200):** carrying out or performing

• **forbidden (p. 201):** not allowed

• **eligible (p. 201):** qualified

• **fugitives (p. 203):** people who escape

• **furnishing (p. 204):** supplying

ORGANIZING INFORMATION Fill in the chart below to illustrate federal, state, and concurrent powers.

EVALUATING INFORMATION Mark each statement *T* if it is true or *F* if it is false.

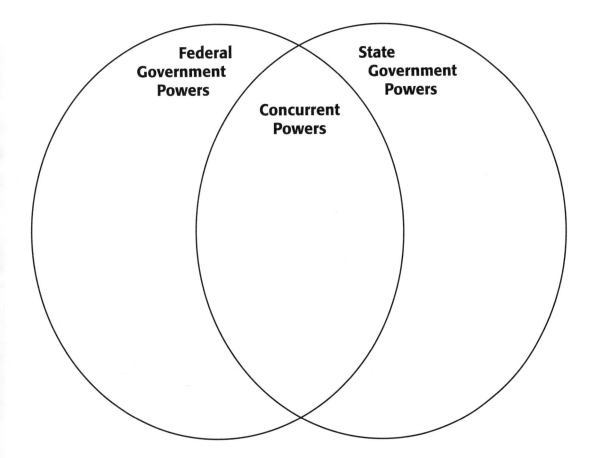

Chapter 8, Main Idea Activities 8.1, continued

_____ **1.** The Articles of Confederation allowed each state to issue its own money.

_____ **2.** Only the federal government can regulate trade between the states.

_____ **3.** The U.S. Virgin Islands are now considered a state.

_____ **4.** In order to become a state, a territory must write a state constitution to be approved by the people of the territory and Congress.

_____ **5.** Each state has the right to refuse to accept the decisions of courts in other states.

_____ **6.** States rarely cooperate on projects that affect them both.

_____ **7.** It is the responsibility of each state to find a way to protect itself if the country is attacked.

_____ **8.** One example of a concurrent power is the power of taxation.

_____ **9.** A marriage certificate issued by one state is accepted by all other states.

_____ **10.** Hawaii was the last state to join the union.

REVIEWING FACTS Choose the correct terms from the following list to complete the statements below.

    territories   concurrent powers
    full faith and credit clause   extradition

1. If a fugitive from Texas has fled to Connecticut, he or she can be returned to Texas

based upon the method of _____.

2. The power to collect state and federal taxes is an example of

_____.

3. The _____ ensures that each state will accept official records of any other state.

4. Puerto Rico, Guam, American Samoa, and the U.S. Virgin Islands are examples of

U.S. _____.

Name _____ Class _____ Date _____

VOCABULARY Some terms to understand:

• **sparsely (p. 206):** lightly

• **adopted (p. 207):** accepted

ORGANIZING INFORMATION Complete the diagram below by identifying and defining the three processes through which citizens can be involved in lawmaking and elections.

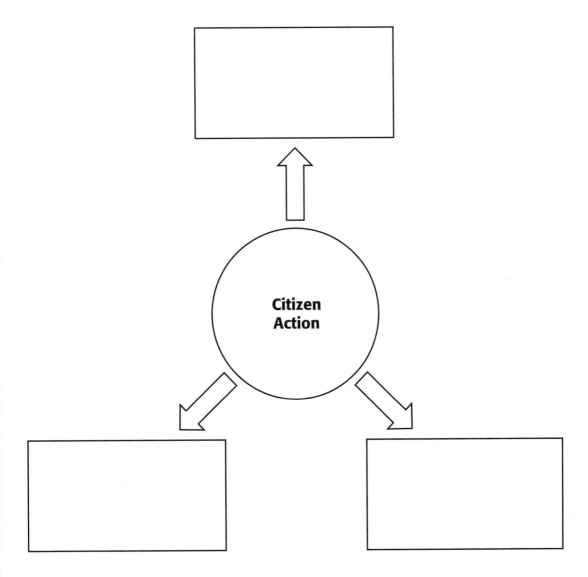

Chapter 8, Main Idea Activities 8.2, continued

EVALUATING INFORMATION Mark each statement *T* if it is true or *F* if it is false.

_____ **1.** All states have a bicameral legislature.

_____ **2.** Almost all states require that members of a state legislature live in the district they represent.

_____ **3.** All state senators and representatives are elected for four-year terms.

_____ **4.** In most states, the lieutenant governor presides over the Senate.

_____ **5.** Hardly any work of the state legislatures is done in committees.

_____ **6.** State legislatures may vote to pass a bill, change it, or kill it.

_____ **7.** Only if both houses pass a bill in the same form can it be sent to the governor to be signed.

_____ **8.** A bill may be sent to a joint-conference committee so that both houses can reach a compromise.

UNDERSTANDING MAIN IDEAS For each of the following, write the letter of the best choice in the space provided.

_____ **1.** If a legislature is unicameral, it has
   a. one house.
   b. two houses.
   c. three houses.
   d. four houses.

_____ **2.** If a governor kills only one part of a bill, he or she has performed a(n)
   a. referendum.
   b. initiative.
   c. item veto.
   d. recall.

_____ **3.** If voters create a petition for a recall, it means that they would like to remove a(n)
   a. bill.
   b. law.
   c. elected official.
   d. none of the above.

_____ **4.** Legislatures vary in
   a. size.
   b. qualifications for members.
   c. salaries for members.
   d. all of the above.

CHAPTER **8**   Main Idea Activities 8.3

State Government

VOCABULARY Some terms to understand:

- **residence (p. 213):** where one lives
- **outlines (p. 213):** summarizes or makes a rough draft of
- **oppose (p. 213):** to be against
- **issue (p. 213):** to give out
- **budget (p. 213):** a financial plan
- **policies (p. 214):** guidelines or procedures
- **resigns (p. 215):** quits
- **vacant (p. 215):** empty
- **prosecution (p. 215):** trial
- **authorized (p. 215):** allowed
- **measures (p. 216):** actions

ORGANIZING INFORMATION Fill in the puzzle pieces with four of the powers and duties of governors.

Powers and Duties of Governors:

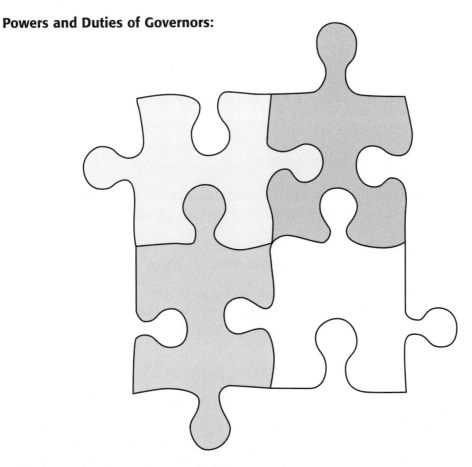

Chapter 8, Main Idea Activities 8.3, continued

EVALUATING INFORMATION Mark each statement *T* if it is true or *F* if it is false.

_____ **1.** Every governor is the chief executive of his or her state.

_____ **2.** All governors serve four-year terms.

_____ **3.** The secretary of state keeps state records and carries out election laws.

_____ **4.** The superintendent of public instruction is in charge of handling all state funds.

_____ **5.** Every state has a governor's cabinet.

_____ **6.** State governments do not usually employ many people.

_____ **7.** The voters of each state elect officials such as lieutenant governor and secretary of state.

_____ **8.** A state's department of public works is responsible for all public construction projects in the state, including work done on interstate highways.

REVIEWING FACTS Choose the correct terms from the following list to complete the statements below.

governor   warrant
executive orders patronage
lieutenant governor

1. The treasurer cannot pay any bills without the written order signed by the auditor

called a(n) _____.

2. A state's executive branch is headed by the _____.

3. Some state jobs are filled through _____, or giving the jobs to people who are recommended by political party leaders and officeholders.

4. The _____ of a state becomes head of the state executive branch if the governor dies, resigns, or is removed from office.

5. The orders that set up methods of enforcing laws are called

_____.

Name _____ Class _____ Date _____

VOCABULARY Some terms to understand:

- **welfare (p. 217):** well-being or safety
- **violations (p. 217):** breaking the rules
- **disputes (p. 217):** disagreements or arguments
- **misdemeanors (p. 218):** wrongdoings
- **consent (p. 220):** agreement
- **overburdened (p. 220):** having too much work, care, or responsibility
- **efficiently (p. 221):** well-organized
- **pressing (p. 221):** urgent or important

ORGANIZING INFORMATION Fill in each gavel below to identify the names and duties of courts within the system.

Chapter 8, Main Idea Activities 8.4, continued

REVIEWING FACTS Choose the correct terms from the following list to complete the statements below.

penal code	complaint	municipal courts
criminal cases	plaintiff	small claims courts
civil cases	justice of the peace	general trial courts

1. In a civil case, the person filing the lawsuit is the _____.

2. _____ handle major criminal and civil cases.

3. _____ deal with disputes between individuals or businesses.

4. A _____ hears minor cases in rural areas and small towns.

5. A set of criminal laws is referred to as a _____.

6. Special courts that hear civil cases involving small amounts of money are called

_____.

7. A _____ is another word for a lawsuit.

8. _____ involve people who violate the law by harming individuals or the community.

9. _____ are usually divided into smaller courts that handle specific types of cases.

CLASSIFYING INFORMATION For each of the following, write the letter of the type of court that would handle the situation.

_____ **1.** a traffic violation

_____ **2.** a murder trial

_____ **3.** A person is suing another for $1,000.

_____ **4.** A person is found guilty and has already appealed. This court is his or her last chance.

_____ **5.** A person has been found guilty and disagrees.

_____ **6.** A person is accused of stealing $10,000.

a. lower court

b. general trial court

c. appeals court

d. state supreme court

Name _____ Class _____ Date _____

VOCABULARY Some terms to understand:

- **corporations (p. 223):** businesses or companies
- **economical (p. 224):** cheap or inexpensive
- **supervise (p. 224):** to oversee or control
- **rely (p. 224):** to depend on
- **regulating (p. 226):** controlling

ORGANIZING INFORMATION Write a short description of what each county official does below his or her picture.

EVALUATING INFORMATION Mark each statement *T* if it is true or *F* if it is false.

Sheriff
_____
_____
_____

County Clerk
_____
_____

County Treasurer
_____
_____

County Auditor
_____
_____

District Attorney
_____
_____

Chapter 9, Main Idea Activities 9.1, continued

_____ **1.** All local governments receive their powers from the state governments.

_____ **2.** Local government provides residents with trash collection and running water.

_____ **3.** Local governments do not usually work with state governments.

_____ **4.** Every state has 200 counties.

_____ **5.** The county form of government was formed within the past 100 years.

_____ **6.** County governments help the state government collect state taxes and conduct elections.

_____ **7.** The group of officials at the head of a county government is elected by Congress.

_____ **8.** The traditional form of county government has been successful in all areas of the country.

REVIEWING FACTS Choose the correct terms from the following list to complete the statements below.

charters	counties	county clerk
municipality	county seat	district attorney
ordinance	sheriff	

1. A(n) _____ is a regulation that governs the community.

2. The role of a(n) _____ is to keep records of births, deaths, election results, and marriages.

3. Most local governments receive _____, or basic plans for local government, from the state.

4. In the southern colonies, plantation owners of each county met regularly in a centrally located town known as the _____.

5. The role of a(n) _____ is to enforce the law.

6. A(n) _____, which is established by petition and election by residents, includes cities, villages, and boroughs.

7. A(n) _____ represents the state government in county trials.

8. Most states are divided into parts, or _____.

Name _____ Class _____ Date _____

VOCABULARY Some terms to understand:

• **influential (p. 228):** powerful or important

• **outlying (p. 228):** far-off or distant

• **moderator (p. 230):** a go-between who helps opposing people or groups to communicate

• **preside (p. 230):** to supervise or direct

• **sufficient (p. 232):** enough

• **permits (p. 233):** allows

ORGANIZING INFORMATION Fill in the chart below to compare towns, townships, and villages.

	Towns	**Townships**	**Villages**
Definition			
How government works today			

EVALUATING INFORMATION Mark each statement *T* if it is true or *F* if it is false.

_____ **1.** Counties are the largest unit of local government.

_____ **2.** In town meetings of early New England towns, representatives chosen by citizens decided what was best for the town.

_____ **3.** Early township governments maintained local roads and rural schools.

_____ **4.** In the Middle Atlantic states, township governments eventually transformed into county-township governments.

_____ **5.** People called constables enforce laws within a township government system.

_____ **6.** Special districts are the least numerous of the country's local governments.

Chapter 9, Main Idea Activities 9.2, continued

_____ **7.** Special districts meet many needs, such as fire protection and public transportation.

_____ **8.** People may establish a village or borough form of government without approval from the state legislature.

_____ **9.** A village may collect taxes and set up fire and police protection.

_____ **10.** In order for a place to be considered a city, it must have a certain population.

_____ **11.** Early towns and villages differed only in population.

_____ **12.** Town officials include a town clerk, members of the school board, and a tax collector.

UNDERSTANDING MAIN IDEAS For each of the following, write the letter of the best choice in the space provided.

_____ **1.** Special districts may provide all of the following needs EXCEPT
   a. libraries.
   b. parks.
   c. air travel.
   d. education.

_____ **2.** Of the following four types of governments, which serves the largest population?
   a. towns
   b. cities
   c. boroughs
   d. villages

_____ **3.** Congressional townships were prevalent in the
   a. Northeast.
   b. Middle Atlantic.
   c. Midwest.
   d. Southwest.

_____ **4.** Townships mainly serve what types of areas?
   a. rural
   b. suburban
   c. urban
   d. all of the above

CHAPTER **9**   Main Idea Activities 9.3

Local Government

VOCABULARY Some terms to understand:

• **relatively (p. 234):** somewhat

• **authority (p. 234):** power

• **duplication (p. 235):** repeating

• **consent (p. 237):** approval or permission

• **adopted (p. 238):** took on or accepted

• **adequate (p. 238):** enough

• **jurisdiction (p. 238):** control or power

CLASSIFYING INFORMATION For each of the following, write the letter of the correct choice in the space provided.

_____ **1.** Mayor has chief responsibility for running the city's government.

_____ **2.** City is governed by elected officials.

_____ **3.** Resulted from early colonists' experience with British governors who did not listen to them

_____ **4.** Voters elect a city council to make laws.

_____ **5.** Mayor draws up a city budget.

_____ **6.** City is run by specially trained professionals.

_____ **7.** The city council holds more power than the mayor.

_____ **8.** City managers are appointed, not elected.

_____ **9.** The mayor must obtain the consent of council before taking action.

_____ **10.** Includes department heads of public safety

_____ **11.** First set up in South Carolina in 1912

_____ **12.** Mayor appoints most city officials.

a. weak-mayor plan

b. strong-mayor plan

c. commission government

d. council-manager government

Chapter 9, Main Idea Activities 9.3, continued

EVALUATING INFORMATION Mark each statement *T* if it is true or *F* if it is false.

_____ **1.** The city government is responsible for education, but not health and safety.

_____ **2.** A city government may take one of three forms: a mayor-council government, a commission government, or a council-manager government.

_____ **3.** The oldest and most common form of city government is the commission government.

_____ **4.** Under a strong-mayor plan, mayors can hire and dismiss city officials.

_____ **5.** One disadvantage of commission government is that sometimes commissioners disagree as to which department should manage certain activities.

_____ **6.** City governments do not necessarily need to receive charters from state legislatures.

_____ **7.** The mayor is appointed by the city council.

_____ **8.** Two types of mayor-council governments are the weak-mayor plan and the strong-mayor plan.

REVIEWING FACTS Choose the correct terms from the following list to complete the statements below.

city   commission
home rule   wards
city council   council members at large

1. A city has the power to write and amend its own municipal charter under

_____.

2. When all voters in a city choose each council member in a mayor-council government, the officials are referred to as _____.

3. _____ is the lawmaking body of the mayor-council government.

4. Under the mayor-council form of government, a city is divided into several districts,

or _____.

5. A _____ is usually larger than a town or village.

6. A city may be governed by a _____ in which three to nine elected officials act as the lawmaking and executive body.

Main Idea Activities 9.4

Local Government

VOCABULARY Some terms to understand:

- **conflict (p. 241):** disagree or clash
- **rutted (p. 242):** bumpy
- **contribute (p. 242):** to put in or add to
- **industries (p. 244):** businesses
- **distinguish (p. 244):** to figure out

ORGANIZING INFORMATION Fill in the graphic organizer below with examples that illustrate the ways in which local, state, and federal governments work together.

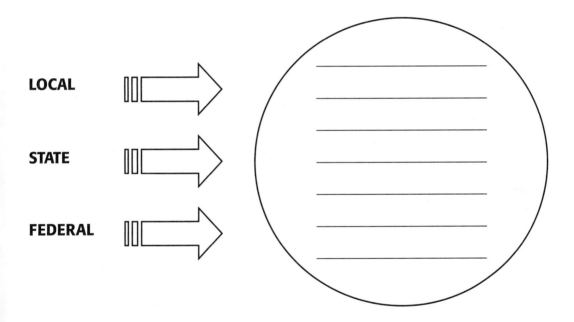

Chapter 9, Main Idea Activities 9.4, continued

EVALUATING INFORMATION Mark each statement *T* if it is true or *F* if it is false.

_____ **1.** Building roads has always been a cooperative effort among local, state, and federal governments.

_____ **2.** State governments grant funds to communities to help them operate schools.

_____ **3.** The federal government provides school lunch programs for students from low-income families.

_____ **4.** Local and state police do not usually cooperate with the FBI to capture suspects.

_____ **5.** Block grants are defined as federal funds given to state and local governments for specific projects.

_____ **6.** Only some city governments are concerned about increasing funds for education.

_____ **7.** Fire alarms that go off in a certain neighborhood may only be answered by the neighborhood's fire department.

_____ **8.** Governments compete with one another.

_____ **9.** The federal government may challenge state election procedures if such procedures conflict with a new federal law.

_____ **10.** The United States felt a need for large roads and highways connecting the East to the West because the country was expanding.

_____ **11.** For a long time, local governments and private companies built most of the roads in the United States.

_____ **12.** Actual control of schools is left to the federal government.

Main Idea Activities 10.1

Electing Leaders

VOCABULARY Some terms to understand:

- **favors (p. 253):** prefers or supports
- **voluntary (p. 253):** doing something by choice
- **campaigns (p. 254):** running for election
- **ensure (p. 254):** to make certain of
- **establishment (p. 255):** creation
- **unheeded (p. 255):** unrecognized
- **benefit (p. 255):** to help
- **stable (p. 256):** constant

ORGANIZING INFORMATION Complete the chart below to show how political parties in the United States have evolved.

First Political Parties	Political Parties in the 1820s–today	Examples of Third Parties

EVALUATING INFORMATION Mark each statement *T* if it is true or *F* if it is false.

_____ **1.** Political parties are voluntary in all countries.

_____ **2.** U.S. citizens must join a political party.

_____ **3.** President George Washington believed that political parties were dangerous and could divide the country.

_____ **4.** In 1854, the Republican Party opposed slavery.

_____ **5.** Governments that have a one-party system are usually dictatorships or totalitarian governments.

_____ **6.** Once a person joins a political party, he or she cannot leave that party.

Chapter 10, Main Idea Activities 10.1, continued

_____ **7.** Thomas Jefferson led the Democratic-Republican Party.

_____ **8.** Several European countries have more than two strong political parties.

_____ **9.** Theodore Roosevelt ran for president under the Progressive Party.

_____ **10.** Benito Mussolini of Italy ran a government of three strong political parties.

REVIEWING FACTS Choose the correct terms from the following list to complete the statements below.

political party	two-party system	third party
nominate	multiparty system	one-party system
candidates	coalition	

1. Political parties _____, or select, men or women to run for public office.

2. Countries such as Cuba and North Korea have governments based on a

_____.

3. In the Netherlands, two or more political parties work together to run the government and have a _____.

4. A _____ is an organization made up of citizens who have similar ideas on public issues.

5. The United States has a _____ involving the Democrats and Republicans.

6. Theodore Roosevelt and Ross Perot ran for office under a _____.

7. _____ are defined as men and women who run for election to offices at various levels of the government.

8. Many European countries have a _____, or one in which there are more than two strong political parties.

Name _____ Class _____ Date _____

VOCABULARY Some terms to understand:

- **expenses (p. 259):** the cost of operating or running
- **enlarged (p. 260):** increased
- **distributes (p. 260):** gives out
- **conduct (p. 260):** to carry out
- **prominent (p. 260):** well-known or important
- **harmony (p. 260):** agreement
- **monitor (p. 262):** to observe or look after

ORGANIZING INFORMATION Complete the chart below to show how political parties in the United States have evolved.

	National Committee	**State Central Committees**	**Local Committees**
How members are chosen			
What it does			

EVALUATING INFORMATION Mark each statement *T* if it is true or *F* if it is false.

_____ **1.** Candidates running for election may raise as much money as they can from any source they want.

_____ **2.** All citizens of the United States must contribute to the Presidential Election Campaign Fund.

_____ **3.** Precincts make voting easier for citizens and more efficient for election officials.

_____ **4.** Precinct captains distribute information about a campaign and get to know people in the neighborhood.

_____ **5.** It is difficult to monitor how campaign contributions are actually spent.

UNDERSTANDING MAIN IDEAS For each of the following, write the letter of the best choice in the space provided.

_____ **1.** The size of a precinct can be
   a. the length of a few city blocks.
   b. a large area of a countryside.
   c. an entire town.
   d. all of the above.

_____ **2.** The Federal Election Campaign Act passed in 1972 requires that political candidates
   a. may keep the identities of contributors confidential.
   b. may accept any amount of money from contributors.
   c. report the names of people who contribute more than $200 in a year.
   d. report the names of people who contribute more than $100 in a year.

_____ **3.** In order to receive public funds for a campaign, a candidate must
   a. win the election.
   b. raise $5,000 from private contributions.
   c. raise less than $5,000 from private contributions.
   d. be approved to do so by Congress.

_____ **4.** Each of the following are examples of party committees EXCEPT the
   a. National Committee.
   b. State Central Committee.
   c. City Committee.
   d. Local Committee.

Main Idea Activities 10.3

Electing Leaders

VOCABULARY Some terms to understand:

- **roll (p. 265):** list
- **resemble (p. 267):** to look like or to be similar to

EVALUATING INFORMATION Mark each statement *T* if it is true or *F* if it is false.

_____ **1.** A person must be no less than 21 years of age to vote in most states.

_____ **2.** Any U.S. citizen of voting age can vote.

_____ **3.** Most states require voters to register before the day of an election.

_____ **4.** A person must register as a member of a political party.

_____ **5.** Usually two separate elections are held in most states—the primary and general elections.

_____ **6.** Delegates are people who attend and vote in a nominating convention.

_____ **7.** It is rare that a person be elected to office by write-in votes.

_____ **8.** In general, independent candidates are elected more often than major-party candidates.

_____ **9.** The president and members of Congress are elected in odd-numbered years.

_____ **10.** People of the community work as inspectors, or poll watchers, within a polling place.

_____ **11.** Almost all states use the paper ballot.

_____ **12.** In many states, the law provides that all employers must give time off during the day to any employee who wants to vote.

_____ **13.** The Voting Rights Act passed in 1965 states that in order to vote, one must be literate.

_____ **14.** Those people who have registered as independent voters cannot vote in a closed primary.

Chapter 10, Main Idea Activities 10.3, continued

REVIEWING FACTS Choose the correct items from the following list to complete the statements below.

independent voters	closed primary	grassroots support	split ticket
primary election	open primary	secret ballots	
general election	runoff	straight ticket	

1. In a(n) _____, only those voters who are registered in the party can vote to choose the party's candidates.

2. Independent candidates usually receive _____ in which many individuals at the local level support the candidate.

3. The _____ allows voters to choose the candidates from each party who will run in the later **4.** _____.

5. If no candidate receives a majority, a(n) _____ between the two leading candidates decides the winner.

6. Voters who are not members of a political party may register as

_____.

7. In a(n) _____, voters may vote for the candidates of either major party, whether or not the voters belong to that party.

8. _____ allow voters to keep who they vote for confidential.

9. If voters choose to vote for candidates of more than one political party, they are

voting a(n) _____.

10. If you were to vote for all Democrats, you would be voting a(n)

_____.

UNDERSTANDING MAIN IDEAS For each of the following, write the letter of the best choice in the space provided.

_____ **1.**
X Jones (D)
X Smith (R)
X Brown (D)

The ballot above shows
a. a split ticket.
b. a straight ticket.
c. a mixed ticket.
d. none of the above.

_____ **2.** All of the following are current methods used to vote EXCEPT
a. punchcards.
b. DRE systems.
c. lever machines.
d. voice voting.

CHAPTER **10**   Main Idea Activities 10.4

Electing Leaders

VOCABULARY Some terms to understand:

- **platform (p. 271):** beliefs
- **vast (p. 271):** very large
- **heated (p. 272):** intense or passionate
- **endorse (p. 272):** to support

ORGANIZING INFORMATION Number the following steps in this example of an election process.

_____

| Electoral votes are sent to the president *pro tempore* of Senate. |

_____

| House of Representatives chooses president |

_____

| Discover that no candidate receives majority of votes. |

_____

| Citizens cast their vote for president. |

_____

| Electors gather and cast the state's electoral votes. |

_____

| Electoral votes are counted |

Chapter 10, Main Idea Activities 10.4, continued

EVALUATING INFORMATION   Mark each statement *T* if it is true or *F* if it is false.

_____ **1.** Electors are not required to vote for their party's candidate.

_____ **2.** In the presidential election, Americans do not vote directly for the president.

_____ **3.** At national nominating conventions, people agree on a party's platform and nominate presidential and vice presidential candidates.

_____ **4.** A woman has never been nominated for the vice presidency.

_____ **5.** During the election campaign, candidates usually stay close to home and work on strategies.

REVIEWING FACTS   Choose the correct items from the following list to complete the statements below.

    presidential primaries   popular vote   electoral college
    party platform   electors   electoral votes
    favorite sons or daughters

1. A(n) _____ is a written statement that outlines a party's views on important issues and sets forth a proposed program for the nation.

2. The _____ refers to the votes cast by citizens.

3. In _____, voters indicate which candidate they want the delegates to vote for at the national nominating convention.

4. The_____ is made up of 538 members.

5. Party leaders who are popular in their home states are referred to as

_____.

6. A candidate must win the _____ to become president.

7. _____ cast the official votes for president.

CHAPTER 11

Main Idea Activities 11.1

The Political System

VOCABULARY Some terms to understand:

- **transmit (p. 280):** to send out or pass on
- **inaccurate (p. 280):** incorrect
- **favorable (p. 280):** positive or approving
- **critically (p. 280):** rationally or logically
- **endorsements (p. 282):** approval
- **vague (p. 283):** unclear
- **representative (p. 284):** typical

ORGANIZING INFORMATION Fill in the appropriate terms or definitions below.

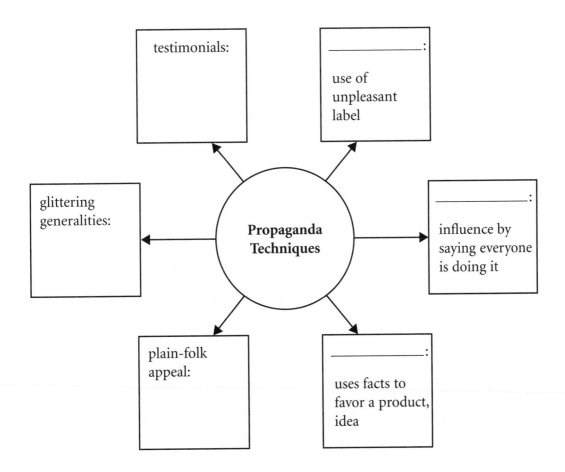

Chapter 11, Main Idea Activities 11.1, continued

EVALUATING INFORMATION Mark each statement *T* if it is true or *F* if it is false.

_____ **1.** Public opinion refers to one opinion.

_____ **2.** Our family and the media shape our opinions.

_____ **3.** Growth of the mass media and advances in technology have decreased the amount of propaganda.

_____ **4.** Both a representative and unrepresentative sample of people yield the same results.

_____ **5.** Sometimes people may respond a certain way to a poll so that they appear to support a winner.

_____ **6.** Testimonials often involve famous people.

REVIEWING FACTS Choose the correct terms from the following list to complete the statements below.

public opinion	concealed propaganda
mass media	revealed propaganda
propaganda	poll

1. _____ makes readers or listeners aware that someone is trying to influence them.

2. Using a _____, or survey, is one way to measure public opinion.

3. _____ is defined as the total of the opinions held concerning a particular issue.

4. In general, spreading ideas to influence people is called _____.

5. Forms of _____ include newspapers, television, radio, films, books, and magazines.

6. _____ is information that is presented as being factual while its sources are kept secret.

VOCABULARY Some terms to understand:

- **consumers (p. 288):** customers
- **staff (p. 288):** workers or employees
- **supply (p. 289):** to provide
- **testify (p. 289):** to give evidence
- **evidence (p. 290):** proof

ORGANIZING INFORMATION Lobbyists use a number of different methods to promote the actions they seek. Think of three examples of what a lobbyist might say to promote his or her beliefs, and fill in the callout boxes.

Chapter 11, Main Idea Activities 11.2, continued

EVALUATING INFORMATION Mark each statement *T* if it is true or *F* if it is false.

_____ **1.** Interest groups attempt to influence the government as well as public opinion.

_____ **2.** Public interest groups seek to promote one part of the general public's interests.

_____ **3.** Interest groups differ in size and budgets, but not goals.

_____ **4.** Most lobbyists work independently and have little or no staff.

_____ **5.** One example of an issue many interest groups struggle over is the minimum wage law.

_____ **6.** Lobbyists are not required to reveal to the government who they work for and how much money they spend in lobbying.

_____ **7.** Business associations, labor unions, and teachers' associations are all kinds of interest groups.

_____ **8.** Lobbyists were once viewed with a great deal of suspicion.

UNDERSTANDING MAIN IDEAS For each of the following, write the letter of the best choice in the space provided.

_____ **1.** All of the following groups represent the economic interests of their members EXCEPT
  a. the American Farm Bureau Federation.
  b. the National Organization for Women.
  c. the United Mine Workers of America.
  d. the National Association of Manufacturers.

_____ **2.** Perhaps the most important job of a lobbyist is to:
  a. argue in support of bills.
  b. argue against bills.
  c. ask members of Congress to sponsor or reject bills.
  d. supply lawmakers with information.

_____ **3.** In order to influence public opinion, interest groups might
  a. place ads in mass media.
  b. promise to help government officials in elections.
  c. urge people to send letters to public officials.
  d. all of the above.

CHAPTER **11**

Main Idea Activities 11.3

The Political System

VOCABULARY Some terms to understand:

- **vital (p. 291):** very important
- **preservation (p. 291):** protection
- **tallies (p. 292):** counts
- **projections (p. 292):** predictions
- **distribute (p. 294):** to hand out
- **prohibited (p. 294):** not allowed

ORGANIZING INFORMATION You have decided to volunteer your time to help in the upcoming election. Fill in your calendar below with specific jobs you may perform as a volunteer. Plan five activities, one per day.

Sunday	Monday	Tuesday	Wednesday	Thursday	Friday	Saturday
1	2	3	4	5	6	7
8	9	10	11	12	13	14

EVALUATING INFORMATION Mark each statement *T* if it is true or *F* if it is false.

_____ **1.** Almost every American citizen votes in elections.

_____ **2.** Interest groups are prohibited by law from contributing money directly to candidates.

_____ **3.** It is extremely difficult to contact a public official.

_____ **4.** Citizen involvement hinders democracy.

_____ **5.** Volunteers usually get paid for their work.

_____ **6.** People fail to vote because of apathy or illness.

_____ **7.** One person's vote does not count.

_____ **8.** In 1916, election results indicated that Charles Evans Hughes would win the presidency, and he did.

_____ **9.** In 2000, Al Gore won the popular vote over George W. Bush, but he did not win the election.

_____ **10.** You must be 18 years old to vote.

_____ **11.** The number of political action committees has decreased in recent years.

_____ **12.** When people vote for certain candidates, they are expressing their opinions about the candidates' leadership and programs that they support.

_____ **13.** Government officials in the United States are selected by a small percentage of the country's people.

_____ **14.** Interest groups may provide volunteers to help candidates who are sympathetic to their causes.

Name _____ Class _____ Date _____

Paying for Government

VOCABULARY Some terms to understand:

• **account for (p. 300):** make up

• **portion (p. 300):** section or part

• **urgency (p. 301):** need

• **priority (p. 301):** main concern

• **burden (p. 301):** load or trouble

• **trademark (p. 302):** brand name

ORGANIZING INFORMATION Fill in the web diagram below with reasons that explain why the cost of running the government is so high.

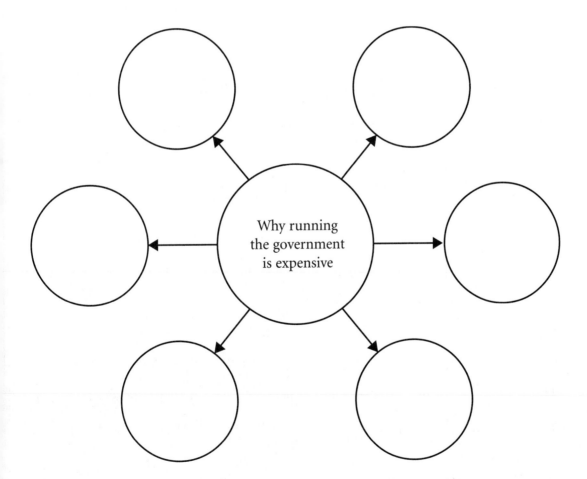

Chapter 12, Main Idea Activities 12.1, continued

EVALUATING INFORMATION Mark each statement *T* if it is true or *F* if it is false.

_____ **1.** Citizens and businesses are not required to pay taxes.

_____ **2.** Government officials must decide which activities need funding more quickly because there is not enough money to fund all of them.

_____ **3.** Taxes on imports and cigarettes are high in part to discourage their use.

_____ **4.** All citizens pay the same amount of taxes, regardless of income.

_____ **5.** The federal government sets April 15 as the deadline for tax payment.

_____ **6.** Governments borrow money by issuing bonds.

_____ **7.** The government does not have to pay interest on the money it borrows.

_____ **8.** Some people disagree about the amount of taxes they pay.

_____ **9.** During the 1990s, the government spent less money on defense.

_____ **10.** Almost everyone agrees on the country's priorities.

REVIEWING FACTS Choose the correct terms from the following list to complete the statements below.

interest   fees
national debt   fines
revenue   bond

1. Small payments called _____ are charged for types of licenses.

2. Illegal parking, speeding, and other traffic violations may result in

_____.

3. The total amount of money plus interest that the U.S. government has borrowed is

called the _____.

4. _____, or money raised by taxes, pays the costs of government.

5. _____ is the payment made for the use of borrowed money.

6. A government _____ is a certificate stating that the government has borrowed a certain sum of money from its owner.

CHAPTER **12**

Main Idea Activities 12.2

Paying for Government

VOCABULARY Some terms to understand:

- **forward (p. 305):** to send on
- **corporation (p. 305):** a business or company
- **controversy (p. 307):** disagreement or debate
- **heirs (p. 307):** children
- **deceased (p. 307):** dead
- **manufacture (p. 308):** to make or produce

ORGANIZING INFORMATION Complete the chart below.

Type of Tax	What is Taxed
Sales tax	
Excise tax	
	Value of property owned by a person or business
Inheritance tax	
	A gift worth more than $10,000
Income tax	
Estate tax	
	Part of a worker's income to be paid for retired people and people with disabilities

REVIEWING FACTS Choose the correct terms from the following list to complete the statements below.

exemption	progressive tax	real property
deductions	profit	personal property
taxable income	regressive tax	tariff

1. A(n) _____ is a tax that takes a larger percentage of income from higher-income groups than from lower-income groups.

Chapter 12, Main Idea Activities 12.2, continued

2. Land, buildings, and other structures are examples of _____.

3. The import tax that the U.S. government collects on products imported from foreign

countries is called a(n) _____.

4. A(n) _____ is the amount of money a taxpayer may subtract
from his or her tax payment for each of their dependents.

5. _____ is the income a business has left after paying its
expenses.

6. A(n) _____ is a tax that takes a larger percentage of income
from lower-income groups than from higher-income groups.

7. _____ is the amount left after all subtractions are made from
total income.

8. Stocks, bonds, jewelry, cars, and boats are examples of _____.

9. Taxpayers can claim charitable contributions and most business expenses as

_____.

EVALUATING INFORMATION Mark each statement *T* if it is true or *F* if it is false.

_____ **1.** The largest source of revenue for the federal government is income taxes.

_____ **2.** The amount of income tax that people pay changes.

_____ **3.** Taxes are taken out of one's income only once a year.

_____ **4.** State and city governments do not collect individual income taxes.

_____ **5.** Social Security tax paid by each worker is matched by the employer.

_____ **6.** Excise taxes are collected on things like gasoline and luxury automobiles.

_____ **7.** The amount taxed for personal property is usually very high.

_____ **8.** Much of the funding for public schools in the United States comes from local
property taxes.

CHAPTER 12

Main Idea Activities 12.3

Paying for Government

VOCABULARY Some terms to understand:

- **manage (p. 310):** to direct or control
- **authorization (p. 311):** approval or permission
- **forecasts (p. 312):** predicts

ORGANIZING INFORMATION Correctly number the boxes to illustrate how a federal budget is prepared.

Congress makes changes to budget.	Executive departments estimate money to be spent.

President approves the final budget.	President and OMB create budget.

Senate and House of Representatives receive budget.

Name _____ Class _____ Date _____

Chapter 12, Main Idea Activities 12.3, continued

EVALUATING INFORMATION Mark each statement *T* if it is true or *F* if it is false.

_____ **1.** After tax money is collected, it is sent to the treasuries of the various governments.

_____ **2.** A comptroller is responsible for ensuring that public funds are spent only as authorized by the president.

_____ **3.** The legislative branch must turn the budget into law before any public money can be spent.

_____ **4.** The function of managing funds is divided between the judicial and legislative branches of government.

_____ **5.** The U.S. government rarely has a deficit.

_____ **6.** A balanced budget occurs when a government's revenue equals its expenditures.

_____ **7.** There is no constitutional limit on the size of the national debt.

_____ **8.** National debt has decreased over time.

UNDERSTANDING MAIN IDEAS For each of the following, write the letter of the best choice in the space provided.

_____ **1.** Social Security taxes are collected by
   a. state governments.
   b. the Internal Revenue Service.
   c. local governments.
   d. the U.S. Treasury Department.

_____ **2.** Which of the following must approve the federal budget?
   a. president
   b. Senate
   c. House of Representatives
   d. all of the above

_____ **3.** The Office of Management and Budget
   a. spends federal tax dollars.
   b. passes the budget as law.
   c. evaluates the effectiveness of executive agencies.
   d. audits expenditures of local governments.

_____ **4.** A budget does all of the following EXCEPT
   a. lists the amount of expected revenue.
   b. specifies how much money is to be spent for various public purposes.
   c. states consequences for failing to pay taxes.
   d. covers the government's operations for one year.

CHAPTER 13 — Main Idea Activities 13.1
Citizenship and the Family

VOCABULARY Some terms to understand:

- **undergone (p. 323):** experienced
- **typical (p. 323):** usual
- **evidence (p. 323):** proof
- **assets (p. 324):** benefits
- **preserve (p. 324):** to maintain or keep from going rotten
- **vast (p. 325):** huge
- **consumed (p. 325):** ate or used
- **trends (p. 326):** developments or tendencies
- **necessity (p. 327):** requirement or need
- **pursue (p. 327):** to go after
- **domain (p. 327):** area or realm

ORGANIZING INFORMATION Complete the chart below to illustrate the four major trends affecting American families and the reasons behind each trend.

Trend	Cause(s) of trend

Chapter 13, Main Idea Activities 13.1, continued

EVALUATING INFORMATION Mark each statement *T* if it is true or *F* if it is false.

_____ **1.** In the past few decades, the American family has undergone many changes.

_____ **2.** Colonial families tended to be smaller than modern American families.

_____ **3.** In colonial days, families themselves produced most of what they needed to survive.

_____ **4.** Families began moving to cities in the 1800s because the children no longer wanted to work on a farm.

_____ **5.** The average age at first marriage for women has decreased over the years.

_____ **6.** Within colonial families, children often got married and brought their spouses to live on the family farm.

_____ **7.** Hardly any children worked in factories in the 1800s.

_____ **8.** As people began moving to cities, families had to rely more on outside sources for food and education.

REVIEWING FACTS Choose the correct terms from the following list to complete the statements below.

delayed marriage   remarried

two-income family   blended families

single-parent families

1. If one or both married partners have been married before, then they have

_____.

2. A family in which both partners work is referred to as a _____.

3. More than 27 percent of American families with children under the age of 18 are

_____.

4. _____ occur when one or both partners bring children from previous relationships into a new marriage.

5. Marrying at an older age is also called a _____.

Main Idea Activities 13.2

Citizenship and the Family

VOCABULARY Some terms to understand:

• **regulate (p. 329):** to control

• **consent (p. 329):** permission or approval

• **hasty (p. 330):** quick or speedy

• **testify (p. 330):** to give evidence

• **violated (p. 330):** break or go against

• **custody (p. 332):** being in charge of

ORGANIZING INFORMATION Fill in the boxes to illustrate the reasons a court may intervene in a marriage or in a home with children.

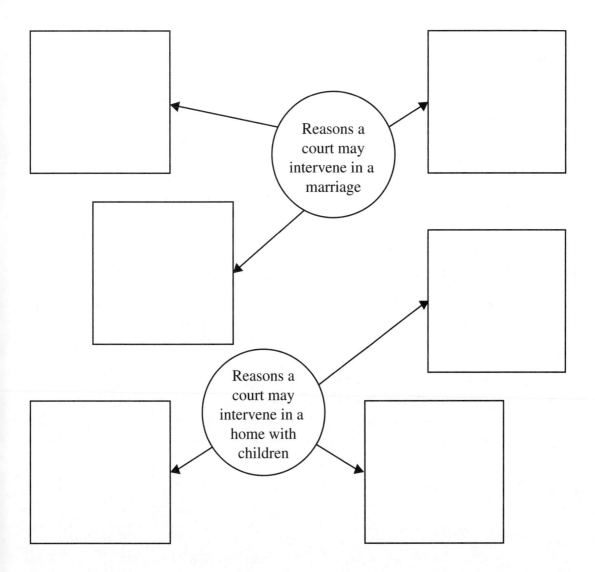

Chapter 13, Main Idea Activities 13.2, continued

EVALUATING INFORMATION Mark each statement *T* if it is true or *F* if it is false.

_____ **1.** There are few laws protecting the rights of families.

_____ **2.** About half the states require that couples wait for one to five days before a marriage license is issued.

_____ **3.** Most states allow people of any age to marry.

_____ **4.** Foster homes are defined as the homes of people who are related to children and agree to act as their caregiver.

_____ **5.** When one adopts a child, one legally establishes the child to be his or her own.

_____ **6.** Social scientists say that one reason for the high divorce rate is that the divorce process has become less complicated over the past few decades.

UNDERSTANDING MAIN IDEAS For each of the following, write the letter of the best choice in the space provided.

_____ **1.** Couples who divorce must make the following decision:
  a. division of property
  b. custody of children
  c. child support payments
  d. all of the above

_____ **2.** A divorce may be defined as
  a. a person appointed by a state court to care for a child.
  b. a final legal ending of a marriage.
  c. emotional, physical, or sexual abuse.
  d. the legal process through which a child is established as one's own.

_____ **3.** Family law regulates all of the following EXCEPT
  a. marriage.
  b. divorce.
  c. birth of a child.
  d. rights of adults and children.

_____ **4.** In most states, a person must be what age to marry?
  a. 16
  b. 18
  c. 21
  d. no age requirement

CHAPTER **13** Main Idea Activities 13.3

Citizenship and the Family

VOCABULARY Some terms to understand:

- **ideal (p. 335):** perfect or model
- **sincere (p. 335):** honest or truthful
- **effectively (p. 336):** well or successfully
- **crises (p. 336):** disasters
- **traits (p. 336):** qualities or characteristics
- **operate (p. 336):** to function

ORGANIZING INFORMATION Fill in the boxes below with some of the expenses a family must pay.

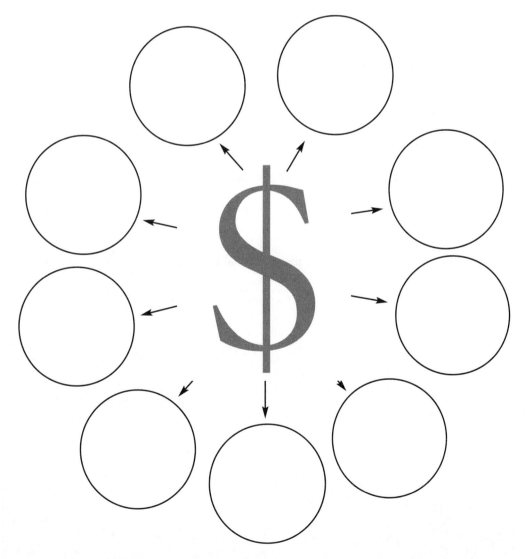

EVALUATING INFORMATION Mark each statement *T* if it is true or *F* if it is false.

_____ **1.** A child's earliest ideas of right and wrong are taught in the home.

_____ **2.** Some parents give their children an allowance to teach them financial responsibilities.

_____ **3.** Most families live in an ideal home that is constantly loving and secure.

_____ **4.** If family members do not work together to find solutions to problems, problems may develop into crises.

_____ **5.** Many families choose not to operate on a budget.

_____ **6.** Fixed expenses are those expenses that occur only once in a while.

_____ **7.** To prepare for the future, you can help your family follow a budget plan.

_____ **8.** The home is usually the best place to learn about home management.

_____ **9.** The family serves the country because it teaches good behavior and good citizenship, and educates its members.

_____ **10.** Using self-restraint and considering other people's points of view help prevent serious conflict.

_____ **11.** Each person has rights.

_____ **12.** Conflicts rarely occur between parents.

_____ **13.** Many disagreements are solved properly by one person giving into the other's demands.

_____ **14.** Budgets usually mean complicated bookkeeping and "pinching pennies."

CHAPTER **14** | Main Idea Activities 14.1

Citizenship in School

VOCABULARY Some terms to understand:

- **access (p. 342):** right to use
- **initially (p. 342):** at first or to begin with
- **funds (p. 343):** money
- **recognition (p. 344):** ability to identify
- **advances (p. 344):** increase or progress
- **income (p. 345):** money earned
- **gifted (p. 346):** very talented
- **enrichment (p. 346):** developing skills even further
- **entitled (p. 346):** allowed
- **fund (p. 348):** support with money
- **reform (p. 348):** to change

ORGANIZING INFORMATION Complete the chart below to illustrate the pros and cons of public education according to people in the 1600s through the 1900s.

Pros	Cons

EVALUATING INFORMATION Mark each statement *T* if it is true or *F* if it is false.

_____ **1.** Americans believe that only some citizens should be given the opportunity to study and learn in order to develop their talents and abilities.

_____ **2.** The first major step in developing public education was taken in Rhode Island in 1647.

_____ **3.** *Kindergarten* in German means "garden for children."

_____ **4.** Some schools have replaced junior high schools with middle schools.

_____ **5.** The three kinds of high schools are academic, technical, and vocational.

_____ **6.** Citizens are entitled to a free public education from kindergarten through high school.

_____ **7.** The Supreme Court allows that school-sponsored prayer shall be allowed during the school day.

_____ **8.** American students' science, math, and reading test scores are lower at most levels than those in other industrial countries.

REVIEWING FACTS Choose the correct terms from the following list to complete the statements below.

community colleges   graduate school
colleges   mainstreaming
university

1. A _____ contains one or more colleges.

2. Junior colleges, or _____, offer two-year degrees.

3. Most _____ offer four-year degrees in a variety of fields.

4. _____ occurs when students with disabilities attend regular classes for most of the day.

5. If one wants an advanced degree, he or she would attend

_____.

Name _____ Class _____ Date _____

VOCABULARY Some terms to understand:

- **foundation (p. 350):** groundwork or base
- **index (p. 352):** directory of terms that indicates what pages certain words appear on
- **glossary (p. 352):** dictionary
- **appendices (p. 352):** additional information added to a text
- **captions (p. 352):** description below a picture
- **admission (p. 353):** entrance or access

ORGANIZING INFORMATION Fill in each of the folders below with tips on how to get the most from your textbooks.

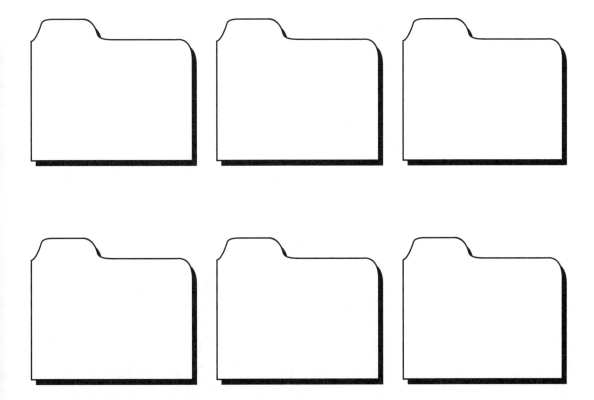

EVALUATING INFORMATION Mark each statement *T* if it is true or *F* if it is false.

_____ **1.** In the 1800s an organization of teachers, parents, and school officials created a list of educational goals for U.S. schools.

_____ **2.** Schools aim to teach reading, writing, arithmetic, and citizenship.

Chapter 14, Main Idea Activities 14.2, continued

_____ **3.** One key goal of your school activities is that you learn to work independently and not within groups.

_____ **4.** Reviewing notes with other students before a test is helpful.

_____ **5.** The success you enjoy in school and the study and learning habits you develop do not play a role in the kind of person you will become.

_____ **6.** Organization is very important in becoming a good student.

_____ **7.** Your school introduces you to good books, art, and music so that they may enrich your life.

UNDERSTANDING MAIN IDEAS For each of the following, write the letter of the best choice in the space provided.

_____ **1.** All of the following are education goals for U.S. schools EXCEPT
   a. health education.
   b. learning to work with others.
   c. learning to take advantage of others to succeed.
   d. active citizenship.

_____ **2.** When taking a test, what is one thing you should not do?
   a. Rush through so that you do not run out of time.
   b. Read each question carefully.
   c. Look over the entire test.
   d. Reread your answers.

_____ **3.** Which of the following may be considered an extracurricular activity?
   a. math class
   b. family dinners
   c. English class
   d. drama club

_____ **4.** When studying, you should
   a. find a noisy area to increase your concentration.
   b. find a dark area to make sure you really pay attention.
   c. take notes while you read.
   d. try not to use other materials.

Name _____ Class _____ Date _____

Citizenship in School

VOCABULARY Some terms to understand:

- **observation (p. 354):** watching
- **complex (p. 355):** not simple
- **overflow (p. 355):** excess or run over
- **maturity (p. 355):** wisdom or adulthood
- **distinguish (p. 356):** to tell apart
- **appropriate (p. 357):** proper or correct
- **influence (p. 357):** power over
- **objective (p. 358):** being able to avoid influence
- **acquire (p. 358):** to obtain or get

REVIEWING FACTS Choose the correct items from the following list to complete the statements below.

experience   motivation   critical thinking
conditioning   insight   prejudice
habit   creativity

1. _____ is an opinion that is not based on a careful and reasonable investigation of the facts.

2. _____ is the internal drive that stirs people and directs their behavior and attitudes.

3. Learning in which an action is produced as a result of past experience is called

   _____ .

4. The kind of thinking we do to reach decisions and solve problems is called

   _____ .

5. The ability to find new ways of thinking and doing things is called

   _____ .

6. An action that is performed automatically without thinking is called a(n)

   _____ .

7. _____ is defined as the direct observation of or participation in events.

8. When an answer suddenly springs to mind, you experience _____ .

Chapter 14, Main Idea Activities 14.3, continued

EVALUATING INFORMATION Mark each statement *T* if it is true or *F* if it is false.

_____ 1. In thinking through an issue, it is important to learn to weigh all the evidence.

_____ 2. The simple way to learn the truth about an issue or to solve a problem is through critical thinking.

_____ 3. Much of what we know is learned by looking and listening.

_____ 4. Usually there is only one answer to a question.

_____ 5. Families, teachers, friends, and the mass media influence what we think.

_____ 6. Few people can be impartial all of the time.

_____ 7. A main purpose of education is to teach people life skills.

_____ 8. People never learn by copying or imitating others.

_____ 9. Our society needs to present more information to its citizens.

_____10. Critical thinking involves defining the issue, distinguishing fact from opinion, weighing the evidence, and reaching a conclusion.

_____11. Knowing which solution is most appropriate to the circumstances is an important part of making decisions and solving problems.

_____12. Almost everything we do is learned.

_____13. Schools teach students how to best use information by analyzing and putting facts together and by drawing conclusions about the facts.

_____14. Thinking involves only awareness.

CHAPTER **15**

Main Idea Activities 15.1

Citizenship in the Community

VOCABULARY Some terms to understand:

- **landing (p. 362):** a place along a river where boats may dock
- **prosperous (p. 363):** successful or thriving
- **enterprising (p. 363):** able to invent and be creative
- **climate (p. 365):** weather or environment
- **abundant (p. 365):** plentiful
- **persuade (p. 365):** convince
- **access (p. 365):** right to use
- **classify (p. 366):** to order or put in categories
- **crops (p. 366):** harvest or products farmers grow
- **droughts (p. 367):** when a lack of rain and water occurs

ORGANIZING INFORMATION Fill in the table below to show the five types of communities and their characteristics.

Type of Community	Characteristics

Chapter 15, Main Idea Activities 15.1, continued

EVALUATING INFORMATION Mark each statement *T* if it is true or *F* if it is false.

_____ **1.** Most farms grow the same types of crops, regardless of their locations.

_____ **2.** The waterways of the United States helped determine the location of many cities.

_____ **3.** Most large inland cities grew up at lake ports or along major rivers.

_____ **4.** Many New England communities settled near waterfalls so that the water could be used to create power for factories.

_____ **5.** A community's climate and resources do not affect the types of government services needed by the people living there.

_____ **6.** Many farms in the southern states grow tobacco and cotton.

_____ **7.** There are now two rural Americas.

_____ **8.** In the 1990s only one quarter of all Americans lived in urban communities.

_____ **9.** Many American communities grew because they were located on transportation routes.

_____ **10.** The railroad hindered cities' growth.

REVIEWING FACTS Choose the correct terms from the following list to complete the statements below.

crossroads
metropolitan area
megalopolis

1. A _____, or where two main roads met, was generally a good place to sell supplies to local farmers and travelers.

2. A giant urban area that forms a continuous urban chain is referred to as a

_____.

3. A _____ includes a large city and its surrounding towns and suburbs.

Main Idea Activities 15.2

Citizenship in the Community

VOCABULARY Some terms to understand:

- **ease (p. 369):** to make better or relieve
- **means (p. 369):** way
- **worthwhile (p. 370):** valuable or useful
- **furnish (p. 372):** to supply or provide

ORGANIZING INFORMATION Fill in each of the boxes below with examples of ways people communicate with one another.

Chapter 15, Main Idea Activities 15.2, continued

EVALUATING INFORMATION Mark each statement *T* if it is true or *F* if it is false.

_____ **1.** Recreational facilities should allow people to do interesting and healthful things.

_____ **2.** The people of a community can meet certain needs more effectively by working together.

_____ **3.** Local courts, judges, and law enforcement officers help maintain peace and order in a community.

_____ **4.** Many recreational facilities are not maintained at public expense.

_____ **5.** People may form communities to provide better services to citizens.

_____ **6.** Services such as providing water, a sewage system, and trash removal can only be performed by the local government.

UNDERSTANDING MAIN IDEAS For each of the following, write the letter of the best choice in the space provided.

_____ **1.** One place that provides recreation is
   a. an office building.
   b. a sporting event.
   c. a movie theater.
   d. b and c.

_____ **2.** All of the following are recreational facilities sponsored by groups of citizens EXCEPT
   a. the Girl Scouts.
   b. 4-H Clubs.
   c. school gyms.
   d. YWCA.

_____ **3.** People live in communities to
   a. enjoy the company of others.
   b. live in privacy.
   c. raise their own crops.
   d. none of the above.

_____ **4.** All of the following are forms of communication EXCEPT
   a. newspapers.
   b. telephones.
   c. helicopters.
   d. computers.

CHAPTER 15   Main Idea Activities 15.3

Citizenship in the Community

VOCABULARY Some terms to understand:

- **vital (p. 374):** very important
- **limited (p. 375):** small amount
- **advisory (p. 375):** advice giving
- **staff (p. 375):** workers
- **firearms (p. 375):** guns or weapons
- **disbands (p. 376):** breaks up
- **permanent (p. 376):** lasting
- **specific (p. 376):** particular
- **litter (p. 377):** waste or trash

CLASSIFYING INFORMATION For each of the following, write the letter of the correct choice or choices in the space provided.

_____ **1.** volunteer firefighters

_____ **2.** first-aid volunteers

_____ **3.** student-parent-teacher associations

_____ **4.** League of Women Voters

_____ **5.** group that cleans up the neighborhood

_____ **6.** American Cancer Society

_____ **7.** volunteers to operate special equipment

_____ **8.** library volunteers

_____ **9.** Volunteers of America

_____ **10.** American Red Cross

a. small local group, later disbands

b. permanent volunteer groups in towns, cities, and counties

c. groups that require training

d. national groups

Chapter 15, Main Idea Activities 15.3, continued

EVALUATING INFORMATION Mark each statement *T* if it is true or *F* if it is false.

_____ **1.** No citizenship services are compulsory.

_____ **2.** In the small town of Las Vegas, New Mexico, the community worked towards helping its young people.

_____ **3.** Pittsburgh, Pennsylvania, once had a major problem with pollution.

_____ **4.** Volunteers provide services that a community might otherwise be unable to afford.

_____ **5.** You are not an active member of a community.

_____ **6.** Decatur, Illinois, still struggles with slums and traffic jams because the community could not come together.

_____ **7.** Many cities have begun to rebuild older areas of the city.

_____ **8.** Hospital volunteers are an example of a permanent volunteer group.

_____ **9.** Retired people are unable to volunteer.

_____ **10.** The American Red Cross has more than one million volunteers working for it.

_____ **11.** It is important that you are a good citizen in your local community.

_____ **12.** One responsibility you have is to pick up litter.

_____ **13.** The League of Women Voters is supported by government funds.

_____ **14.** Volunteers may help in schools, libraries, and museums.

CHAPTER 16   Main Idea Activities 16.1

Citizenship and the Law

VOCABULARY Some terms to understand:

- **decade (p. 381):** ten years
- **classified (p. 382):** organized or labeled
- **intention (p. 382):** meaning to do something
- **theft (p. 382):** stealing
- **abandon (p. 382):** to leave behind
- **willful (p. 383):** intentional
- **organization (p. 384):** group
- **undetected (p. 384):** hidden or unknown
- **lenient (p. 385):** merciful or easy on

ORGANIZING INFORMATION Fill in the boxes below to show the four causes of crime.

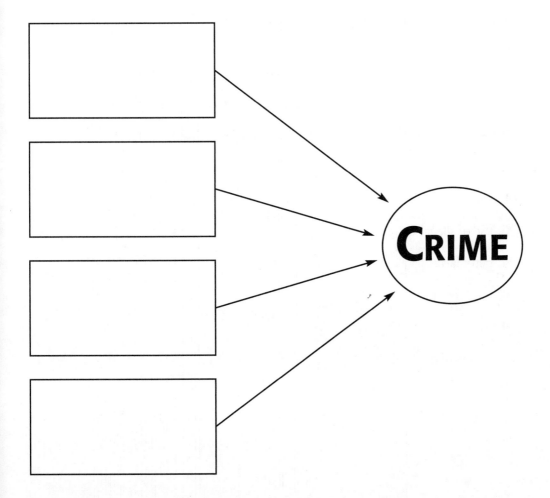

Chapter 16, Main Idea Activities 16.1, continued

EVALUATING INFORMATION Mark each statement *T* if it is true or *F* if it is false.

_____ **1.** The FBI identifies 300 types of crime.

_____ **2.** There are five main crime categories.

_____ **3.** People can commit crimes against other people, but not property.

_____ **4.** The sale and possession of illegal drugs increases the death rate and may lead to other crimes, such as robbery.

_____ **5.** Criminals only act on their own, not within a group.

_____ **6.** Victimless crimes are not so serious because there are no victims.

_____ **7.** The national crime bill passed in 1994 involves life sentences for three-time violent offenders.

_____ **8.** Crime rates have dropped in the past decade.

CLASSIFYING INFORMATION For each of the following, write the letter of the correct crime category in the space provided.

_____ **1.** homicide   **a.** crimes against persons

_____ **2.** burglary   **b.** crimes against property

_____ **3.** embezzlement   **c.** victimless crimes

_____ **4.** arson   **d.** white-collar crimes

_____ **5.** gambling   **e.** organized crimes

_____ **6.** use of illegal drugs

_____ **7.** petty larceny

_____ **8.** forcible rape

_____ **9.** fraud

_____ **10.** aggravated assault

Main Idea Activities 16.2

Citizenship and the Law

VOCABULARY Some terms to understand:

• **duties (p. 387):** responsibilities

• **function (p. 387):** job

• **undue (p. 387):** unnecessary or too much

• **aptitude (p. 388):** ability or skill

• **mobility (p. 388):** ability to move around

• **presumed (p. 391):** assumed or accepted

• **adequate (p. 392):** enough

• **reformed (p. 392):** changed for the better or improved

REVIEWING FACTS Choose the correct terms from the following list to complete the statements below.

criminal justice system	arraigned	acquitted
community policing	defense	plea bargain
probable cause	prosecution	parole

1. A police officer must have _____ to make an arrest; in other words, he or she must have witnessed a crime or gathered enough evidence to make an arrest.

2. In _____, officers are encouraged to get to know the people who live and work in the neighborhood.

3. In a(n) _____, an accused person pleads guilty to a lesser offense than the original charge.

4. The three-part system of police, courts, and corrections used to bring criminals to

justice is known as the _____.

5. Many prisoners may be eligible for _____, or early release.

6. If a person is _____ of a crime, he or she is found not guilty.

7. When a person is _____, he or she enters a plea of guilty or not guilty to a charge.

8. The _____ represents the accused person's side of the case.

9. The _____ presents the government's side of a case in a trial.

EVALUATING INFORMATION Mark each statement *T* if it is true or *F* if it is false.

_____ **1.** Usually the law sets a minimum and maximum penalty for each type of crime.

_____ **2.** The sole purpose of imprisonment is retribution, or revenge.

_____ **3.** All citizens support capital punishment.

_____ **4.** Those training to be police officers must go through a great deal of training.

_____ **5.** When people are arrested, they must be told by the police officer that they have the right to remain silent.

_____ **6.** Immediately after being arrested, a person goes to trial.

UNDERSTANDING MAIN IDEAS For each of the following, write the letter of the best choice in the space provided.

_____ **1.** Which of the following illustrates the correct order of events in the criminal justice system?
  a. arrest, trial, sentencing, imprisonment
  b. trial, arrest, sentencing, imprisonment
  c. arrest, sentencing, trial, imprisonment
  d. imprisonment, sentencing, trial, arrest

_____ **2.** Which of the following is NOT a reason for imprisonment?
  a. deterrence to crime
  b. rehabilitation
  c. education
  d. social protection

_____ **3.** In training to be a police officer, one must
  a. be a certain age.
  b. live in a particular city.
  c. pass physical exams.
  d. all of the above.

_____ **4.** Examine the following police report. Which piece of information does the police officer NOT need to record?

> Arrest Report:
>
> (a) John Smith
> (b) 6:55 P.M.
> (c) Larceny
> (d) Age: 31

Name _____ Class _____ Date _____

Citizenship and the Law

VOCABULARY Some terms to understand:

• **unruly (p. 395):** wild or uncontrollable

• **outlets (p. 396):** means through which one may express feelings

• **reformers (p. 397):** people who work towards change

ORGANIZING INFORMATION Fill in the circles below with ways to avoid criminal behavior.

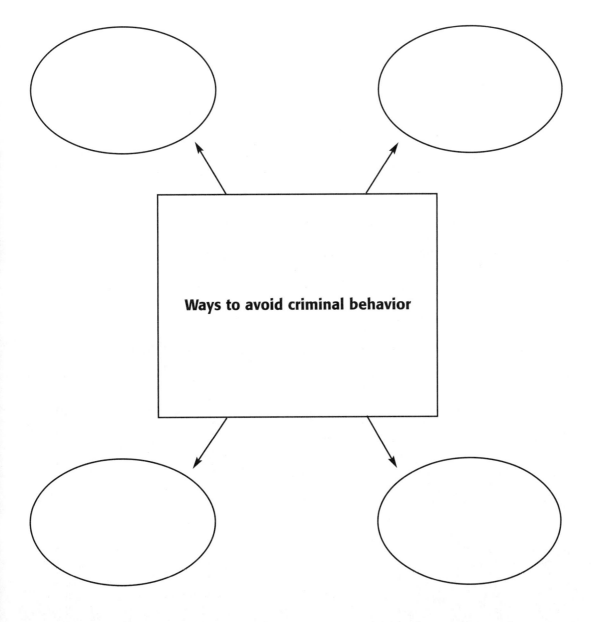

Ways to avoid criminal behavior

Chapter 16, Main Idea Activities 16.3, continued

EVALUATING INFORMATION Mark each statement *T* if it is true or *F* if it is false.

_____ **1.** All states consider juveniles to be young people under the age of 18.

_____ **2.** Juveniles become delinquents when they are found either innocent or guilty of breaking a law.

_____ **3.** Poor home conditions and juvenile crime are not connected.

_____ **4.** Some young people view delinquency and crime as their only way out of poverty.

_____ **5.** Young people who drop out of school and are unemployed are often at greater risk of becoming involved in criminal activities.

_____ **6.** Before the late 1800s, juveniles at least 7 years old were held responsible for their crimes.

_____ **7.** Anyone is allowed to become involved in a juvenile court hearing.

_____ **8.** Juveniles have the right to be informed of the charges brought against them and to be represented by a lawyer.

_____ **9.** Juveniles are never tried before juries.

_____ **10.** In most states, juveniles cannot be tried in adult criminal courts.

_____ **11.** One possible outcome for a juvenile offender is probation.

_____ **12.** More young people have been sentenced to adult prisons in recent years.

_____ **13.** Peer pressure is related to juvenile delinquency.

_____ **14.** Young people are responsible for a small percentage of crime in the United States.

Name _____ Class _____ Date _____

VOCABULARY Some terms to understand:

- **goods (p. 407):** products
- **exclusive (p. 409):** private or restricted
- **resources (p. 409):** a source of supply of support
- **supply (p. 409):** amount
- **demand (p. 409):** what is wanted
- **hand labor (p. 411):** work done by people as opposed to by machines
- **acquire (p. 412):** to get or obtain

ORGANIZING INFORMATION Fill in the diagram below with the names and definitions of the different economic systems.

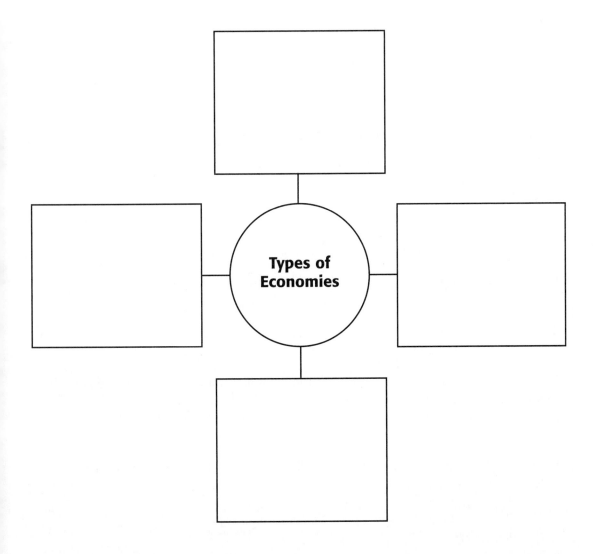

Chapter 17, Main Idea Activities 17.1, continued

EVALUATING INFORMATION Mark each statement *T* if it is true or *F* if it is false.

_____ **1.** The United States has a free economy.

_____ **2.** The law of demand states that businesses will provide fewer products when they must sell them at lower prices.

_____ **3.** Capitalism encourages people to work and to invest.

_____ **4.** The government must enforce rules to control monopolies and trusts.

_____ **5.** All monopolies are legal.

REVIEWING FACTS Choose the correct terms from the following list to complete the statements below.

market economy	invest	monopoly
free competition	law of demand	merger
profit motive	capitalism	conglomerate

1. _____ is a system based on private or corporate ownership of the means of production.

2. A(n) _____ is formed by the merger of businesses that produce, supply, or sell a number of unrelated goods.

3. The _____ states that buyers will demand more products when they can buy them at lower prices.

4. An economy in which people have the freedom to buy and sell what they choose when they choose is called a(n)_____.

5. To _____ in businesses and valuable goods is to put money into them.

6. In a system of _____, each business tries to persuade people to buy what it has to offer.

7. A company is a(n) _____ if it is the only firm selling a product or producing a service.

8. The desire to make a profit is called the _____.

9. A(n) _____ occurs when two or more companies combine to form one company.

CHAPTER **17**

Main Idea Activities 17.2

The Economic System

VOCABULARY Some terms to understand:

• **furnish (p. 418):** to provide

• **entitles (p. 419):** permits or allows

• **oversee (p. 419):** to supervise

REVIEWING FACTS Choose the correct items from the following list to complete the statements below.

sole proprietorships   stocks   preferred stock

partnerships   stockholders   common stock

corporation   dividends   nonprofit organizations

1. Corporation profits paid to people who hold stock are called

_____.

2. People who own _____ receive money only if the company makes a profit.

3. Businesses in which two or more people share the responsibilities, costs, profits, and

losses are known as _____.

4. Small businesses owned by one person are called _____.

5. Owners of _____ take less risk in investing their money, for they are guaranteed a fixed dividend every year.

6. _____ provide goods and services without seeking to earn a profit.

7. A _____ is the most common form of business organization for the country's large companies.

8. People who buy corporate stocks are called _____.

9. _____ are shares of ownership of a corporation.

EVALUATING INFORMATION Mark each statement *T* if it is true or *F* if it is false.

_____ **1.** Corporations receive their rights to operate from state governments.

_____ **2.** Sole proprietorships usually have two to three owners.

_____ **3.** Owners of common stock are at less risk than those who own preferred stock.

Chapter 17, Main Idea Activities 17.2, continued

_____ **4.** If a business fails, the stockholders are responsible for paying a corporation's debts.

_____ **5.** Corporations may issue bonds to gain additional sums of money.

_____ **6.** The directors of corporations are elected by the stockholders.

_____ **7.** Each share of stock entitles its owner to two votes for the board of directors' election.

_____ **8.** The American Red Cross and the American Heart Association are nonprofit organizations.

CLASSIFYING INFORMATION For each of the following, write the letter of the correct choice in the space provided.

_____ **1.** most common form of business organization

_____ **2.** do not have a vote in a company's affairs

_____ **3.** Girl Scouts

_____ **4.** may sell their shares for more than they paid for them

_____ **5.** will not end when owners die

_____ **6.** Smith and Brown, Attorneys

_____ **7.** take less risk in their investment

_____ **8.** have a vote in electing board of directors

_____ **9.** take more risk in their investment

_____ **10.** is not taxed by the government

a. corporation

b. preferred stockholders

c. common stockholders

d. nonprofit organization

e. partnership

CHAPTER **17**

Main Idea Activities 17.3

The Economic System

VOCABULARY Some terms to understand:

• **scarce (p. 423):** in short supply or limited

• **fixed (p. 425):** unchanging

• **prosper (p. 426):** to do well

ORGANIZING INFORMATION Fill in the boxes with some of the roles the government plays in the free-enterprise system.

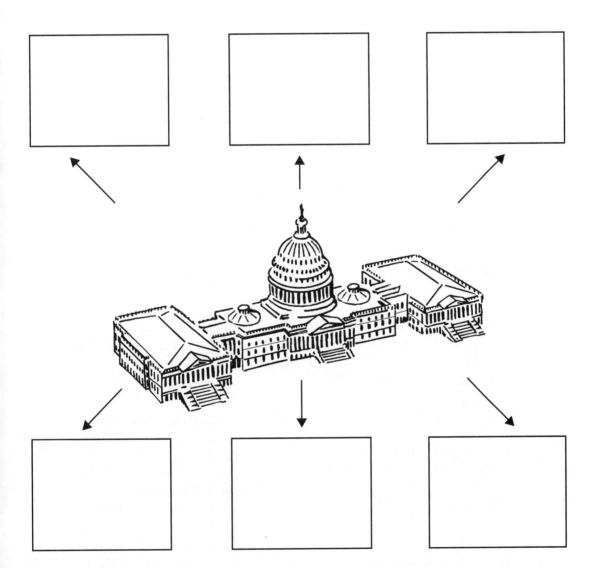

EVALUATING INFORMATION Mark each statement *T* if it is true or *F* if it is false.

_____ **1.** A natural resource is considered a factor of production only when it is plentiful.

_____ **2.** Entrepreneurs who run businesses are called managers.

_____ **3.** The word labor is often used to mean workers as opposed to owners and people who manage companies.

_____ **4.** The amount left over after all costs have been paid is called gross income.

_____ **5.** Some people believe that the government has gone too far in doing its job as an overseer.

_____ **6.** Rents and land prices in crowded business areas where land is scarce are lower than in less densely populated areas.

_____ **7.** Examples of capital are trucks, machines, and office equipment.

_____ **8.** Every business enterprise needs land.

_____ **9.** When entrepreneurs make decisions, they are taking risks.

_____ **10.** Businesses must often raise their prices to cover the costs of meeting government regulations.

UNDERSTANDING MAIN IDEAS For each of the following, write the letter of the best choice in the space provided.

_____ **1.** All of the following are factors of production EXCEPT
  a. labor.
  b. entrepreneurship.
  c. capital.
  d. a board of directors.

_____ **2.** Which of the following does the government NOT have a right to do?
  a. protect workers from discrimination
  b. tell businesses who to hire
  c. protect buyers from dishonest practices
  d. provide loans to businesses

_____ **3.** Which of the following is a natural resource that may be considered a factor of production?
  a. electricity
  b. air on the beach
  c. ocean water
  d. iron ore

_____ **4.** Management may
  a. make a business prosper.
  b. make a business fail.
  c. make decisions as to how a company will run.
  d. all of the above.

CHAPTER **18**

Main Idea Activities 18.1

Goods and Services

VOCABULARY Some terms to understand:

• **output (p. 431):** amount produced

• **bore (p. 432):** to drill

ORGANIZING INFORMATION Identify and describe the three elements of mass production.

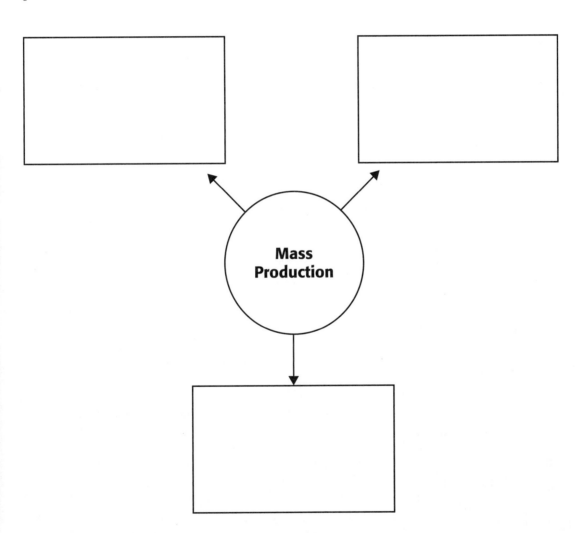

EVALUATING INFORMATION Mark each statement *T* if it is true or *F* if it is false.

_____ **1.** One of the first inventors to make mass production possible was Eli Whitney.

_____ **2.** The source of power that contributed most to modern mass production was waterpower.

_____ **3.** Automobile factories use an assembly line.

_____ **4.** Cuba uses mass production methods but has not been as successful as other countries due to its command economy.

_____ **5.** Economists use the GDP as the only measure of how well the U.S. economy is performing.

_____ **6.** Mass production is used to produce radios and tractors.

_____ **7.** Mass production was first developed in England.

_____ **8.** Mass production is quicker than making products by hand.

REVIEWING FACTS Choose the correct terms from the following list to complete the statements below.

gross domestic product   interchangeable parts

mass production   division of labor

machine tools   assembly line

1. In _____, each worker is responsible for a specific task in production.

2. A(n) _____ uses machines and workers to move a product through stages of production until it is completed.

3. The _____ refers to the dollar value of all goods and services produced annually in the United States.

4. _____ are made to be identical so that they can replace other parts.

5. _____ is defined as the rapid production by machine of large numbers of identical objects.

6. _____ are types of machinery built to produce parts that are exactly the same.

CHAPTER **18**   Main Idea Activities 18.2

Goods and Services

VOCABULARY Some terms to understand:

• **canal (p. 437):** inland waterway

• **freight (p. 437):** goods

• **bulk (p. 438):** a product in large amounts

• **emission (p. 439):** discharge

• **standard (p. 440):** typical

• **complexes (p. 441):** development or set of buildings

• **prosperity (p. 441):** wealth

• **persuade (p. 442):** to convince

ORGANIZING INFORMATION Fill in the chart below.

Distribution method	Increase or decrease in use	Disadvantages to method

REVIEWING FACTS Choose the correct items from the following list to complete the statements below.

distribution	standard packaging	retailers
mass marketing	one-price system	advertising
self-service	wholesaler	brand name

1. A(n) _____ product is widely advertised and distributed.

2. In a(n) _____, prices are stamped or bar-coded onto products.

Chapter 18, Main Idea Activities 18.2, continued

3. A(n) _____ is a businessperson who owns a large warehouse where goods are stored.

4. _____ is the process of moving goods from manufacturers to the people who want them.

5. Selling goods in large quantities is called _____.

6. _____ sell goods directly to the public.

7. _____ is an efficient and inexpensive way to sell goods because it saves time and labor.

8. _____ informs people about products and tries to persuade them to buy these products.

9. _____ means that goods come from factories already wrapped.

EVALUATING INFORMATION Mark each statement *T* if it is true or *F* if it is false.

_____ **1.** A chain store is owned and operated by a company that has many of the same kind of stores.

_____ **2.** A factory often sells goods to a wholesaler who then sells them to retailers.

_____ **3.** Transportation was important to the United States because it unified the country.

_____ **4.** U.S. trains are faster than trains in other countries.

_____ **5.** The airplane is the leading means of transportation in the United States.

_____ **6.** Many tracks and trains in the United States are in poor condition.

CHAPTER **18**

Main Idea Activities 18.3

Goods and Services

VOCABULARY Some terms to understand:

• **slogan (p. 443):** a saying or motto

• **allowance (p. 444):** amount one is allowed

• **mislead (p. 446):** to give the wrong impression about

ORGANIZING INFORMATION Imagine that you are about to buy a computer. Fill in the boxes below with the three payment options you have.

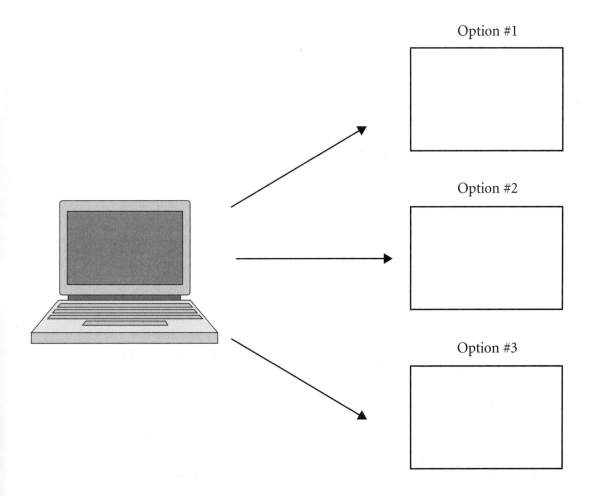

Option #1

Option #2

Option #3

EVALUATING INFORMATION Mark each statement *T* if it is true or *F* if it is false.

_____ **1.** The government requires that labels be put on certain products, but does not dictate what information should be on the labels.

_____ **2.** Shoplifting hardly hurts a business.

Chapter 18, Main Idea Activities 18.3, continued

_____ **3.** Anyone can open a charge account, regardless of his or her past credit history.

_____ **4.** If a customer makes late or incomplete payments on a product, the seller can repossess the item.

_____ **5.** A consumer is a person who buys or uses goods and services.

_____ **6.** Many consumers avoid shopping at well-known stores because products are more expensive.

_____ **7.** Some laws require that products show unit pricing on their label.

_____ **8.** There is no protection for consumers when they discover that products have been falsely labeled or advertised.

_____ **9.** Shoplifting can eventually cause consumers to pay more for products and services.

_____ **10.** Charge accounts always offer lower interest rates than banks.

UNDERSTANDING MAIN IDEAS For each of the following, write the letter of the best choice in the space provided.

_____ **1.** All of the following must be on package labels EXCEPT
  a. wholesale cost of item.
  b. package contents.
  c. weight or quantity of items in package.
  d. manufacturer information.

_____ **2.** Which of the following is a consumer protection organization?
  a. Department of the Interior
  b. Department of Agriculture
  c. Department of Defense
  d. Department of Food

_____ **3.** One disadvantage to having a charge account is that
  a. it is easier to keep track of spending.
  b. it is more difficult to return purchases.
  c. customers may buy things on impulse.
  d. none of the above.

_____ **4.** A down payment is defined as
  a. cash used to pay the entire purchase price.
  b. equal payments of a balance.
  c. the rest of what a buyer owes.
  d. cash used to pay part of the purchase price.

CHAPTER  19

Main Idea Activities 19.1
Managing Money

VOCABULARY Some terms to understand:

• **penalties (p. 455):** punishments or consequences

• **deducted (p. 455):** subtracted

• **declare (p. 457):** to state or announce

ORGANIZING INFORMATION Fill in the diagram below with the ways you could pay for the car pictured.

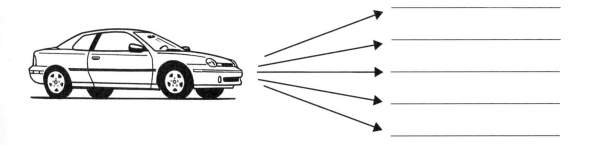

EVALUATING INFORMATION Mark each statement *T* if it is true or *F* if it is false.

_____ **1.** All currency must be easy to carry and take up little space.

_____ **2.** Most coins for general circulation are made in California.

_____ **3.** Today, a nickel is still made of pure nickel.

_____ **4.** Checks are considered legal tender.

_____ **5.** Debit cards operate the same way that checks do.

_____ **6.** Credit can be both very helpful and dangerous.

_____ **7.** To slow consumer spending, banks may extend less credit to customers when production drops.

_____ **8.** People have always used paper money as currency.

_____ **9.** The highest denomination of paper bills is $500.

_____ **10.** Most of what is bought and sold in the United States is paid for with coins and paper money.

Chapter 19, Main Idea Activities 19.1, continued

REVIEWING FACTS Choose the correct terms from the following list to complete the statements below.

money	debit cards	short-term credit
currency	credit cards	long-term credit
check	creditors	bankruptcy

1. _____ can be used at thousands of stores to purchase items without using cash.

2. _____ is also called installment credit.

3. _____ is something that sellers will take in exchange for whatever they have to sell.

4. A _____ is a written and signed order to a bank to pay a sum of money from a checking account to the person or business named on it.

5. If you purchase an item on credit and can repay the debt in a few weeks or months, you only need _____ .

6. Coins and paper money may also be referred to as _____ .

7. _____ are cards that operate the same way that checks do.

8. Those people to whom one owes money are called _____ .

9. _____ is a legal declaration that a person cannot pay his or her debts.

CHAPTER **19**

Main Idea Activities 19.2

Managing Money

VOCABULARY Some terms to understand:

• **chartered (p. 461):** contracted

• **issue (p. 461):** to give out

• **fraud (p. 462):** trick or deception

• **pooled (p. 463):** combined

ORGANIZING INFORMATION Fill in the chart below to compare the four types of banks.

Type of Bank	Services Offered	Money insured by FDIC?

EVALUATING INFORMATION Mark each statement *T* if it is true or *F* if it is false.

_____ **1.** Savings banks began in the early 1800s to encourage savings by people who could make only very small deposits.

_____ **2.** The Federal Reserve System requires that all U.S. banks meet its requirements.

Chapter 19, Main Idea Activities 19.2, continued

_____ **3.** Banking began when people brought their money to goldsmiths for safekeeping.

_____ **4.** Most banks require depositors to keep money in their accounts for a period of time.

_____ **5.** The FDIC insures each depositor's bank account up to $250,000.

_____ **6.** By law, banks cannot turn down a person who seeks a loan from them.

_____ **7.** A loan is rarely renewed.

_____ **8.** A "run" on the bank occurs when rumors spread that a bank is shaky.

_____ **9.** The Federal Reserve System divides the United States into 50 Federal Reserve districts.

_____**10.** If the Federal Reserve wants to speed economic growth, it puts more money into circulation.

UNDERSTANDING MAIN IDEAS For each of the following, write the letter of the best choice in the space provided.

_____ **1.** The Federal Reserve System is managed by
   a. U.S. citizens.
   b. the Senate.
   c. a board of governors.
   d. the president.

_____ **2.** Collateral is defined as
   a. the amount of money needed to be released from jail.
   b. the property used to guarantee that a loan will be repaid.
   c. a business that deals with money and credit.
   d. deducting interest on a loan in advance.

_____ **3.** If a person is refused the renewal of a loan, that person must
   a. immediately pay the money back in full.
   b. take out another loan.
   c. declare bankruptcy.
   d. pay the money back within a year.

_____ **4.** The Federal Reserve banks
   a. handle the banking needs of the federal government.
   b. receive deposits from the secretary of the Treasury.
   c. handle the sale of bonds issued by the government.
   d. all of the above

Main Idea Activities 19.3

Managing Money

VOCABULARY Some terms to understand:

• **maturity (p. 469):** ready to be cashed in

• **via (p. 469):** through

• **expanded (p. 471):** increased

• **consume (p. 471):** to use up

• **prosperous (p. 471):** doing well or thriving

• **monitors (p. 473):** watches closely

CLASSIFYING INFORMATION For each of the following, identify whether the method of saving is relatively low- or high-risk.

_____ **1.** savings account   **a.** low-risk

_____ **2.** stocks   **b.** high-risk

_____ **3.** mutual funds

_____ **4.** bonds

_____ **5.** certificates of deposit

_____ **6.** money-market funds

EVALUATING INFORMATION Mark each statement *T* if it is true or *F* if it is false.

_____ **1.** The only way to tell if your bank is an FDIC or NCUA member is to ask.

_____ **2.** All of the United States' savings organizations come under state or federal supervision.

_____ **3.** When any bond reaches maturity, the holder earns twice the amount paid.

_____ **4.** Stock prices depend on expectations of how well a company will perform in the future.

_____ **5.** The money Americans have in savings accounts helps expand the U.S. economy.

_____ **6.** Saving and investing are the same.

_____ **7.** When you invest, you turn your money into capital.

_____ **8.** All banks must receive a state or federal charter to operate.

_____ **9.** Regular savings accounts usually require a large minimum balance.

_____ **10.** A U.S. savings bond does not pay interest until it is cashed in by the bond-holder.

_____ **11.** Each brokerage house is a member of a stock exchange.

_____ **12.** You can buy stocks from either a brokerage house or over the Internet.

_____ **13.** Stocks always pay more than if the money were invested in a savings account.

_____ **14.** Certificates of deposit allow the holder to withdraw money at any time.

REVIEWING FACTS Choose the correct terms from the following list to complete the statements below.

brokers   certificates of deposit (CDs)
stock exchange   money-market funds
mutual funds

1. _____ buy stocks that most individuals could not purchase alone and allow individuals to withdraw their money at any time.

2. The people employed by brokerage houses are called _____.

3. At the _____, millions of shares of stock are bought and sold every working day.

4. _____ allow savers to invest a certain amount of money for a specified period of time during which time the money cannot be withdrawn.

5. _____ contain many different stocks so that the risk is not so great.

CHAPTER 19

Main Idea Activities 19.4

Managing Money

VOCABULARY Some terms to understand:

- **specify (p. 475):** to state in detail
- **partial (p. 476):** part
- **liability (p. 476):** responsibility
- **segment (p. 478):** part
- **administered (p. 481):** controlled or handed out

ORGANIZING INFORMATION Fill in the diagram below with the names of four types of insurance.

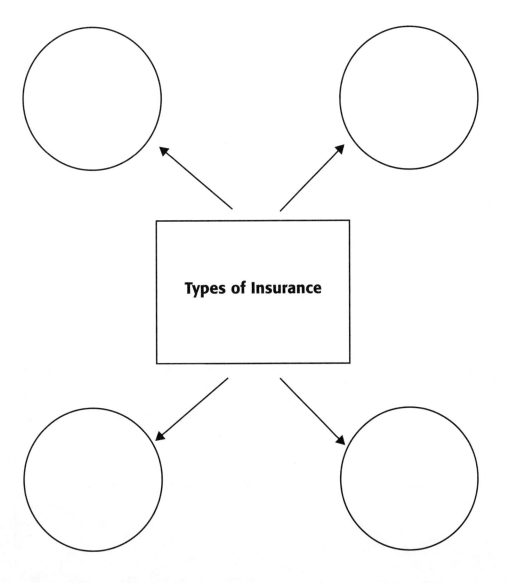

Types of Insurance

Chapter 19, Main Idea Activities 19.4, continued

EVALUATING INFORMATION Mark each statement *T* if it is true or *F* if it is false.

_____ **1.** One type of social insurance is Social Security.

_____ **2.** Medicaid helps U.S. citizens who are 65 or older pay for hospital care and for some nursing-home care.

_____ **3.** The government requires that all citizens have private insurance.

_____ **4.** Insurance fraud may be committed by health-care providers.

_____ **5.** Social Security provides workers with funds once they retire.

_____ **6.** All people receive the same amount in Social Security payments.

_____ **7.** The main purpose of life insurance is to provide the policyholder's family with money in case the policyholder dies.

_____ **8.** Disability income insurance provides payment to workers who have experienced total, not partial, disability.

REVIEWING FACTS Choose the correct terms from the following list to complete the statements below.

insurance	social insurance
premium	beneficiary
private insurance	Medicare

1. Government programs that are meant to protect individuals from future hardship are

called _____.

2. _____ is a system of paying a small amount to avoid the risk of a large loss.

3. The small amount a person pays for insurance is called a(n) _____.

4. _____ is a voluntary insurance that individuals and companies pay to cover unexpected losses.

5. The person named in an insurance policy to receive money when the policyholder

dies is called the _____.

6. _____ helps older citizens pay for hospital care.

CHAPTER  **20**   Main Idea Activities 20.1

Economic Challenges

VOCABULARY Some terms to understand:

- **prosperity (p. 485):** success
- **scarce (p. 486):** in short supply
- **hardships (p. 487):** difficulties
- **restore (p. 489):** to repair or bring back
- **compensation (p. 489):** payment

ORGANIZING INFORMATION Fill in the table below to illustrate whether various factors increase or decrease during an expansion and contraction.

Factors	Expansion	Contraction
Gross domestic product		
Unemployment rate		
Prices		
Business profits		

EVALUATING INFORMATION Mark each statement *T* if it is true or *F* if it is false.

_____ **1.** During a depression, the number of people with jobs is high.

_____ **2.** Before the Great Depression, many economists believed that the government should intervene in the business cycle.

_____ **3.** The Great Depression lasted about a year.

_____ **4.** The FDIC was created as part of the New Deal.

_____ **5.** The business cycle is common to free-market economies.

_____ **6.** During expansion, the cost of doing business increases.

_____ **7.** Increases in prices during an expansion come from an increase in the costs of production.

Chapter 20, Main Idea Activities 20.1, continued

_____ **8.** The Great Depression took place in the 1950s.

_____ **9.** At one point during the Great Depression, business was producing only half as much as it had three years before.

_____ **10.** Before the Great Depression, many economists believed recessions could not last long.

REVIEWING FACTS Choose the correct items from the following list to complete the statements below.

business cycle	costs of production	recession
expansion	peak	trough
inflation	contraction	depression

1. A(n) _____ occurs when the low point of the business cycle is particularly low.

2. The tendency for the economy to go from good times to bad and then back to good times again is called the _____.

3. An economic slowdown is referred to as a(n) _____.

4. When the economy is growing, the country is experiencing a(n) _____.

5. _____ refers to a rise in the costs of goods and services.

6. When the economy reaches its lowest point, it is said to be in a(n) _____.

7. Wages, payments for raw materials, and rent are called the _____.

8. When the expansion of the economy stops, the business cycle has reached its

_____.

9. If a contraction becomes severe, the economy enters a(n) _____.

CHAPTER **20**

Main Idea Activities 20.2

Economic Challenges

VOCABULARY Some terms to understand:

• **pose (p. 490):** to put forward or propose

• **decline (p. 491):** decrease

• **policy (p. 493):** plan

• **aid (p. 493):** help

• **ailing (p. 493):** not well

• **halt (p. 495):** to stop

ORGANIZING INFORMATION Fill in each of the circles below with what economists believe cause economic problems.

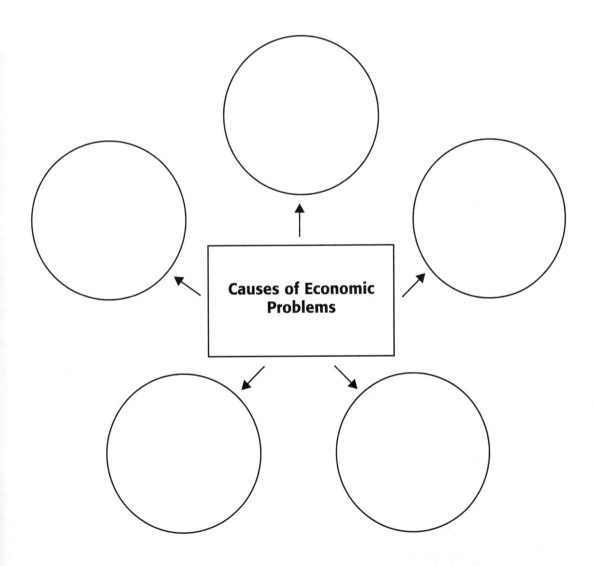

Chapter 20, Main Idea Activities 20.2, continued

EVALUATING INFORMATION Mark each statement *T* if it is true or *F* if it is false.

_____ **1.** Unemployment helps the economy to prosper.

_____ **2.** The government may help slow a recession by reducing taxes.

_____ **3.** When inflation becomes too high, the government may reduce its spending.

_____ **4.** Some economists believe that when the Federal Reserve puts too much money into the economy, prices decrease too much.

_____ **5.** Consumers do not affect the country's economy at all.

_____ **6.** Monetary policy refers to the government's policy regarding money.

_____ **7.** If the total amount produced each hour increases, the supply of goods increases.

_____ **8.** The government must maintain the balance between economic growth and inflation.

UNDERSTANDING MAIN IDEAS For each of the following, write the letter of the best choice in the space provided.

_____ **1.** Citizens can help the economy by
  a. encouraging the government to spend more money.
  b. buying foreign-made products.
  c. increasing their own productivity.
  d. reducing their saving and increasing their spending.

_____ **2.** All of the following decline during recessions EXCEPT
  a. spending.
  b. unemployment.
  c. production.
  d. consumer demand.

_____ **3.** Fiscal policy may be defined as a policy dictating
  a. taxing.
  b. spending.
  c. employment.
  d. a and b

_____ **4.** During a recession, the government might
  a. decrease the money supply.
  b. increase interest rates.
  c. buy government bonds back from banks.
  d. none of the above

VOCABULARY Some terms to understand:

• **unions (p. 498):** organizations in which people join together for a common goal

• **dues (p. 500):** fees for membership

• **enroll (p. 500):** to sign up

• **rivalry (p. 501):** competition

• **collectively (p. 503):** together or in a group

• **revise (p. 503):** to change or improve

• **binding (p. 505):** required

EVALUATING INFORMATION Mark each statement *T* if it is true or *F* if it is false.

_____ **1.** In order to raise money, early labor leaders charged employers dues.

_____ **2.** Because only about 14.9 percent of workers are union members, the American labor unions are weak.

_____ **3.** The Landrum-Griffin Act prohibits convicted criminals from serving as union officials for a period of five years after being released from prison.

_____ **4.** In the first half of the 1800s, factories employed young children as workers.

_____ **5.** A union might demand longer hours for its workers.

_____ **6.** Employers have no options when their workers go on strike.

_____ **7.** The American Federation of Labor and the Congress of Industrial Organizations merged to form a single labor union.

_____ **8.** Unions may compete to see which can get more workers to join.

_____ **9.** When workers go on strike, the only people they affect are their employers.

_____ **10.** The Labor-Management Act is also called the Wagner Act.

_____ **11.** Strikes no longer occur in the United States.

_____ **12.** In the early days of the nation, most Americans were employed by factories.

Chapter 20, Main Idea Activities 20.3, continued

REVIEWING FACTS Choose the correct items from the following list to complete the statements below.

labor unions	picketing	lockouts
collective bargaining	job action	closed shop
strike	blacklists	open shop

1. _____ contained names of workers who were active in the labor unions, and were used to tell other companies not to hire these workers.

2. In _____, representatives of a labor union meet with representatives of an employer to reach an agreement.

3. Organizations of workers hoping to improve wages and working conditions are called

_____.

4. By closing the factory, _____ prevent workers from earning wages.

5. In a(n)_____, union members walk off the job if the employers do not agree to labor's demands.

6. In a(n)_____, workers do not have to be union members or have to join the union to be hired.

7. _____ strikers walk back and forth with signs in front of company buildings, aiming to prevent the hiring of replacement workers.

8. Any kind of slowdown, or action short of a strike, is called a(n) _____.

9. In a(n) _____, workers cannot be hired unless they first become members of the union.

The U.S. Economy and the World

VOCABULARY Some terms to understand:

- **goods (p. 509):** items that may be bought
- **resources (p. 510):** reserves or supplies
- **oversees (p. 510):** supervises
- **exchange (p. 511):** to swap
- **craze (p. 512):** trend

ORGANIZING INFORMATION Fill in the chart below to compare the different types of economies.

TYPE OF ECONOMY	DESCRIPTION

Chapter 21, Main Idea Activities 21.1, continued

EVALUATING INFORMATION Mark each statement *T* if it is true or *F* if it is false.

_____ **1.** Competition does not benefit producers in any way.

_____ **2.** A shortage indicates to producers that they are charging too much for their product.

_____ **3.** Adam Smith believed that self-interest caused the economy to stop growing.

_____ **4.** The United States has a free-enterprise system.

_____ **5.** The U.S. government does not play a role in the U.S. economy.

REVIEWING FACTS Choose the correct terms from the following list to complete the statements below.

producer	circular flow model	supply
human resources	demand	law of supply
capital resources	law of demand	capital goods

1. The _____ dictates that producers supply more goods and services when they can sell them at higher prices.

2. _____ are defined as the labor to produce goods or services.

3. A person or company that produces a good or service that satisfies consumers' needs and wants is called a _____.

4. The _____ dictates that when prices go up, demand drops.

5. _____ is the quantity of goods and services that producers are willing to offer at various possible prices during a given time period.

6. _____ are defined as money used to purchase those things needed to run a business.

7. The _____ demonstrates how the U.S. economy works.

8. _____ is the amount of a good or a service that a consumer is willing to buy at various possible prices during a given time period.

9. Examples of _____ are buildings, machinery, and tools needed to produce items.

The U.S. Economy and the World

VOCABULARY Some terms to understand:

- **external (p. 517):** outside
- **promote (p. 517):** support
- **forecasts (p. 518):** predictions
- **statistics (p. 518):** figures or data
- **prosperity (p. 521):** success or wealth

ORGANIZING INFORMATION Label the graph below with the proper term for each phase of the business cycle.

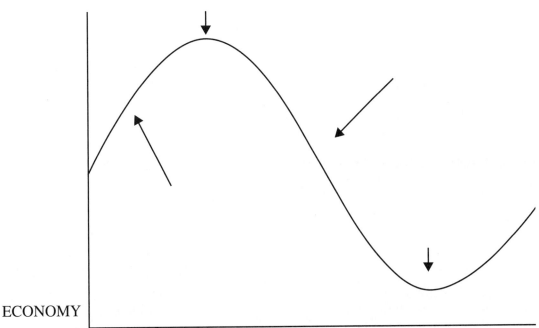

Chapter 21, Main Idea Activities 21.2, continued

EVALUATING INFORMATION Mark each statement *T* if it is true or *F* if it is false.

_____ **1.** Economists are unable to predict changes in the business cycle.

_____ **2.** War influences the U.S. business cycle.

_____ **3.** Business investment promotes economic expansion.

_____ **4.** Lagging indicators change immediately after an upturn or downturn in the economy has started.

_____ **5.** It is cheaper to produce goods in the United States than in any other country.

_____ **6.** A lengthy period of expansion is known as a depression.

_____ **7.** Individuals and businesses generally borrow money when interest rates are low.

_____ **8.** Declining investment makes it more likely that the economy will expand.

_____ **9.** Economists receive information from statistics collected by the U.S. government.

_____ **10.** The events of September 11, 2001, harmed the U.S. economy.

UNDERSTANDING MAIN IDEAS For each of the following, write the letter of the best choice in the space provided.

_____ **1.** Indicators that show economists how the economy is doing at the present time are called
a. lagging indicators.
b. present indicators.
c. coincident indicators.
d. leading indicators.

_____ **2.** All of the following are influences on the business cycle EXCEPT
a. business investment.
b. public opinion.
c. lagging indicators.
d. money and credit.

_____ **3.** The term that describes a high point in the economy is a(n)
a. peak.
b. expansion.
c. trough.
d. recession.

CHAPTER **21**

Main Idea Activities 21.3

The U.S. Economy and the World

VOCABULARY Some terms to understand:

• **network (p. 522):** system

• **exercises (p. 524):** puts into effect

• **banning (p. 524):** forbidding or outlawing

ORGANIZING INFORMATION Fill in the diagram below with the ways the government influences the economy. Include a short description of each method.

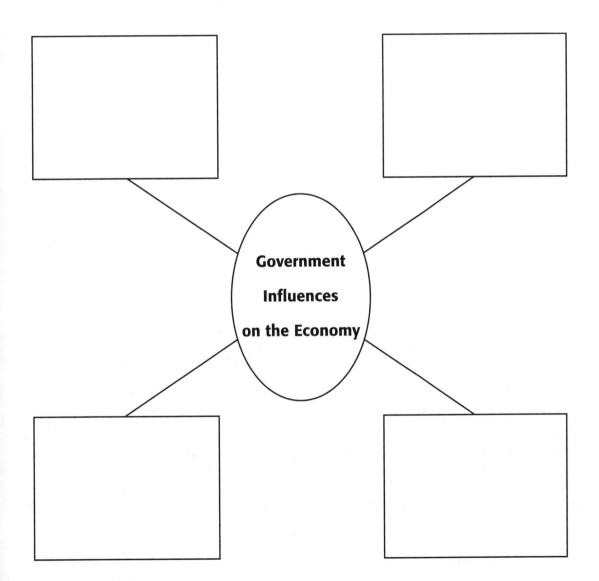

Chapter 21, Main Idea Activities 21.3, continued

REVIEWING FACTS Choose the correct terms from the following list to complete the statements below.

infrastructure   tight-money policy   reserve requirement
tax incentive   open-market operations
easy-money policy   discount rate

1. A(n) _____ is a special tax break.

2. The _____ is the amount of money that banks must have on hand.

3. _____ occurs when the Fed raises interest rates to slow economic growth.

4. The _____ is the network that enables producers and consumers to participate in the economy.

5. A(n) _____ increases the amount of money in the money supply.

6. A(n) _____ is the interest rate that the Fed charges to banks.

7. _____ include the buying and selling of government securities.

EVALUATING INFORMATION Mark each statement *T* if it is true or *F* if it is false.

_____ **1.** If the Fed wants the economy to expand, it lowers the discount rate for banks.

_____ **2.** Negative side effects of economic activities may include pollution and traffic jams.

_____ **3.** Zoning laws allow governments to regulate property.

_____ **4.** To reduce unemployment, the government can reduce its spending.

_____ **5.** The government may lower taxes to increase spending.

_____ **6.** All economists measure the money supply by counting cash, coins, and money in checking accounts only.

_____ **7.** All citizens pay the same amount of income tax, regardless of income.

_____ **8.** The effects of fiscal policy are usually seen immediately.

CHAPTER **21**   Main Idea Activities 21.4

The U.S. Economy and the World

VOCABULARY Some terms to understand:

- **self-sufficiency (p. 529):** the ability to support oneself
- **reciprocal (p. 532):** mutual or give-and-take
- **gradually (p. 532):** slowly
- **efficient (p. 533):** well-organized or capable

ORGANIZING INFORMATION Fill in each box below with the stance of free trade and protectionism supporters on the various issues listed.

ISSUE

Supporters of Free Trade		**Supporters of Protectionism**
	infant industries	
	job protection	
	standard of living	
	specialization	

Chapter 21, Main Idea Activities 21.4, continued

EVALUATING INFORMATION Mark each statement *T* if it is true or *F* if it is false.

_____ **1.** The United States still has an embargo on South Africa.

_____ **2.** Most countries do not support international trade.

_____ **3.** International trade allows countries to specialize.

_____ **4.** International trade helps economies overcome the problem of scarcity.

_____ **5.** Many countries are fully self-sufficient.

REVIEWING FACTS Choose the correct terms from the following list to complete the statements below.

specialize   comparative advantage   trade barrier
interdependence   trade-off
absolute advantage   opportunity cost

1. A(n) _____ is an economic sacrifice.

2. Relying upon other people for some goods and services is known as

_____.

3. A country has a(n) _____ when it can produce a good better than its trading partners can.

4. To _____ means to become good at producing certain kinds of goods.

5. _____ may be defined as the value of the alternative that has been sacrificed during a trade-off.

6. A government action that limits the exchange of goods is called a(n)

_____.

7. Economists determine a(n) _____ by figuring out which product or service offers each nation that greatest absolute advantage.

Main Idea Activities 22.1

Career Choices

VOCABULARY Some terms to understand:

- **suits (p. 541):** matches or goes well with
- **content (p. 542):** satisfied
- **meet (p. 542):** to satisfy or provide for
- **frank (p. 543):** honest

ORGANIZING INFORMATION Under each worker, write a different reason why a person might have chosen that particular career.

EVALUATING INFORMATION Mark each statement *T* if it is true or *F* if it is false.

_____ **1.** The government tells U.S. citizens what profession they ought to pursue.

_____ **2.** The freedom to decide which job to take is sometimes limited by economic conditions.

_____ **3.** Personal values are the things people believe to be the most important in their lives.

_____ **4.** Some people choose a career solely because they can earn a high income.

_____ **5.** An employer expects that his or her employees know everything about a place of business before the employee even begins.

_____ **6.** High-school dropouts typically earn more money as the years pass than those who graduate from high school.

_____ **7.** A person's qualifications ought to match his or her career interests.

_____ **8.** Employers want young men and women who read well, write clearly, and have learned as much as possible in school.

_____ **9.** There is nothing you can do at your age to prepare for a career.

_____ **10.** The most important step in deciding on a career is getting to know yourself.

UNDERSTANDING MAIN IDEAS For each of the following, write the letter of the best choice in the space provided.

_____ **1.** In order to prepare yourself for a career, you must do all of the following EXCEPT
    a. study careers that interest you.
    b. consider the qualities each career requires.
    c. consider government jobs only.
    d. examine your own interests and abilities.

_____ **2.** When reflecting on yourself, consider your
    a. abilities.
    b. strengths.
    c. weaknesses.
    d. all of the above.

Career Choices

VOCABULARY Some terms to understand:

• **manual labor (p. 549):** work performed with the hands

• **assemble (p. 550):** to put together

ORGANIZING INFORMATION Fill in the chart below.

Worker Category	Definition/Examples
Managers, administrators, executives	
	People who sell goods and services
	Biologists, doctors, teachers
Technicians	
Craftspeople	

EVALUATING INFORMATION Mark each statement *T* if it is true or *F* if it is false.

_____ **1.** Today one in every 200 employed Americans is a service worker.

_____ **2.** The need for agricultural workers has increased greatly during the last hundred years.

_____ **3.** White-collar workers make up the largest group of workers in the country today.

_____ **4.** A dental hygienist is an example of a sales worker.

_____ **5.** Most technicians learn their skills in special college courses or in technical or vocational schools.

_____ **6.** Blue-collar workers may work in construction, mining, or transportation industries, among others.

_____ **7.** Each craft has its own labor union that determines the number of people admitted into the craft annually.

_____ **8.** Truck and bus drivers are considered operators.

REVIEWING FACTS Choose the correct terms from the following list to complete the statements below.

white-collar workers	blue-collar workers	automation
professionals	apprenticeship	laborers
technicians	operators	agribusinesses

1. _____ may be defined as the use of machines instead of workers to provide goods and services.

2. People who work in jobs that require many years of education and training and in which the work tends to be mental rather than physical are

_____.

3. Workers who perform jobs that require manual labor are known as

_____.

4. A(n) _____ is a fixed period of on-the-job training.

5. _____ are large farms owned by corporations that rely heavily on mechanized equipment.

6. _____ are people who work in a particular profession or who perform technical, managerial, sales, or administrative support work.

7. _____ are people who perform jobs that require some specialized skill in addition to a solid, basic education.

8. People who operate machines or equipment in factories, mills, industrial plants, gas stations, mines, and laundries are called _____.

9. Workers who perform heavy physical work are called _____.

CHAPTER 22

Main Idea Activities 22.3

Career Choices

VOCABULARY Some terms to understand:

• **extensive (p. 553):** wide-ranging
• **turnover (p. 554):** people leaving their jobs
• **discriminate (p. 554):** to show prejudice
• **upholds (p. 555):** supports or maintains

ORGANIZING INFORMATION Fill in the circles with examples of government jobs.

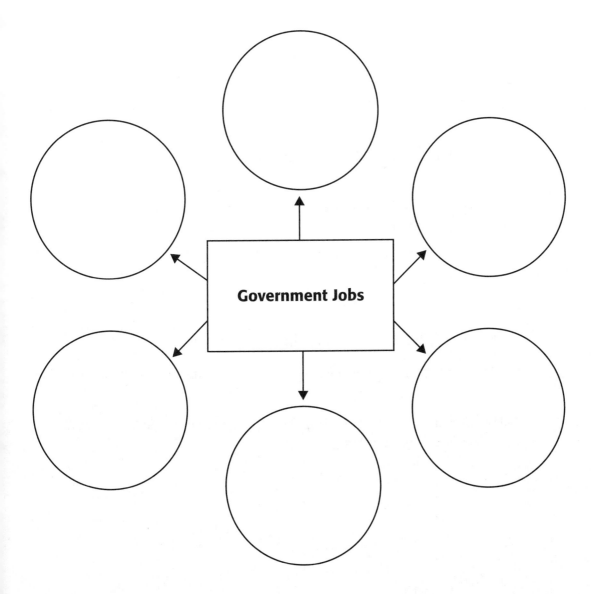

Chapter 22, Main Idea Activities 22.3, continued

EVALUATING INFORMATION Mark each statement *T* if it is true or *F* if it is false.

_____ **1.** The country's largest employer is the U.S. government.

_____ **2.** The child-care and teaching fields will need many more workers over the next 10 years.

_____ **3.** The Civil Rights Acts of 1964 and 1968 helped end discrimination in hiring and wage rates.

_____ **4.** It is wise to focus on and develop skills in only one area.

_____ **5.** Only the federal government, as opposed to state and local governments, employs many different kinds of workers.

_____ **6.** Candidates must be nominated for admission in any of the officer-training academies.

_____ **7.** Every 10 years the U.S. Department of Labor reports where men and women are working and what jobs they are performing.

_____ **8.** Law-enforcement officers and teachers are always in demand.

_____ **9.** The phrase *equal opportunity employer* means that an employer does not discriminate against job applicants because of their sex, age, race, skin color, religion, or ethnic background.

_____ **10.** Most jobs in the military are now open to women.

_____ **11.** Members of the Equal Employment Opportunity Commission are elected by citizens.

_____ **12.** No matter what a person's job is, he or she can always advance.

_____ **13.** Applicants for government jobs typically submit an application like any other type of job.

_____ **14.** Before a candidate is offered a government job, he or she must undergo an extensive background check.

CHAPTER **22**   Main Idea Activities 22.4

Career Choices

VOCABULARY Some terms to understand:

• **guesswork (p. 560):** estimation

• **promptness (p. 560):** being on time

ORGANIZING INFORMATION Choose a job you might be interested in and take the job quiz using the questions listed in the text. Write your answers below.

Job Quiz

Possible Job: _____

1.

2.

3.

4.

5.

6.

7.

Chapter 22, Main Idea Activities 22.4, continued

EVALUATING INFORMATION Mark each statement *T* if it is true or *F* if it is false.

_____ **1.** You can usually look in one place to find the facts you need to choose a career.

_____ **2.** The U.S. Department of Labor publishes the *Occupational Outlook Handbook.*

_____ **3.** It is not a good idea to visit and observe someone in a job you find interesting.

_____ **4.** Baby-sitting is a good job in which you may learn many skills that apply to any job.

_____ **5.** People are usually unable to turn their hobbies into their life's work.

_____ **6.** Reading about career opportunities to find a career that interests you is very straightforward and simple.

_____ **7.** Once you think about a career you might like, try not to change your mind in order to stay focused.

_____ **8.** You may learn about jobs as you go about your daily affairs, making an extra effort to observe teachers, police officers, or office workers.

UNDERSTANDING MAIN IDEAS For each of the following, write the letter of the best choice in the space provided.

_____ **1.** Which of the following statements is NOT true?
    a. the sooner you narrow your career choices the better.
    b. Your interests, talents, abilities, and skills likely will lead you to many career choices.
    c. Learning about careers helps you narrow your choices to careers that will interest you.
    d. You should look at your strengths and weaknesses in making your career choice.

_____ **2.** An important question to ask yourself when thinking about a career is:
    a. What personal qualities does the job require?
    b. What are the job opportunities in this field?
    c. Where will I have to live and work for this kind of job?
    d. all of the above

CHAPTER **22**   Main Idea Activities 22.5

Career Choices

VOCABULARY Some terms to understand:

• **potential (p. 563):** possible

• **chief (p. 564):** main or most important

• **accurately (p. 565):** correctly or exactly

• **interact (p. 566):** to work together

• **seldom (p. 567):** hardly ever

ORGANIZING INFORMATION Complete the job application below based on the four major areas listed in the text.

Job Application

School History:

Health Record:

Outside Activities:

Special Interests:

Chapter 22, Main Idea Activities 22.5, continued

EVALUATING INFORMATION Mark each statement *T* if it is true or *F* if it is false.

_____ **1.** Human resources workers hire or recommend new employees.

_____ **2.** Having a disability should not prevent someone from holding a job.

_____ **3.** One of the most common tests measures a person's ability to work quickly and accurately with numbers.

_____ **4.** An aptitude test can tell you exactly what job you should pursue.

_____ **5.** Most people's first job choice is their final one.

_____ **6.** Schools and private organizations offer aptitude tests and scoring.

_____ **7.** An employer expects that if you are applying for a job, you are able to explain why you believe you are qualified for the job.

REVIEWING FACTS Choose the correct terms from the following list to complete the statements below.

motor skills   interpersonal skills
perceptual skills   aptitude tests

1. _____, or skills in handling personal relationships, are important in teaching and sales.

2. Interest tests are also called _____.

3. The ability to picture things and visualize depth and width from a flat drawing are

referred to as _____.

4. _____ determine how well people can use their hands.

Main Idea Activities 23.1

Foreign Policy

VOCABULARY Some terms to understand:

• **interacts (p. 575):** works together

• **promoting (p. 575):** supporting or encouraging

• **aid (p. 575):** help or assistance

• **advances (p. 575):** developments

• **mutual (p. 575):** shared

• **reliance (p. 575):** dependence

• **consent (p. 576):** permission or approval

• **principal (p. 577):** major or main

• **appointee (p. 577):** someone who is hired or elected

• **surplus (p. 579):** extra

ORGANIZING INFORMATION Fill in the web diagram below to illustrate the goals of U.S. foreign policy.

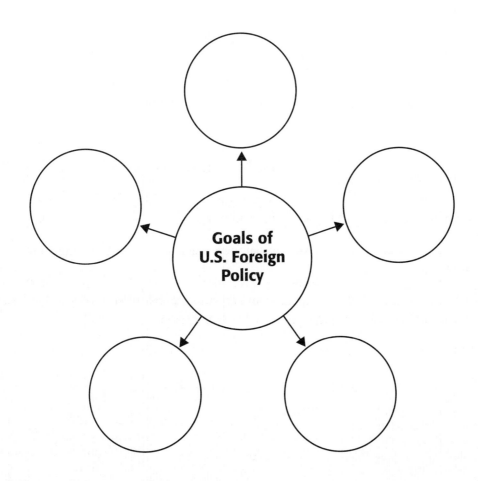

Chapter 23, Main Idea Activities 23.1, continued

EVALUATING INFORMATION Mark each statement *T* if it is true or *F* if it is false.

_____ **1.** The Department of State is the principal organization for carrying out U.S. foreign policy.

_____ **2.** The president does not need approval from the Senate to appoint ambassadors to represent the United States in foreign countries.

_____ **3.** Members of the National Security Council include the president, vice president, and the secretaries of defense, state, and the treasury.

_____ **4.** The House of Representatives must approve all treaties between the United States and other countries by a two-thirds vote.

_____ **5.** Only Congress can declare war.

_____ **6.** The president is the commander in chief of the U.S. armed forces.

_____ **7.** All spending for national defense must be approved by Congress.

REVIEWING FACTS Choose the correct terms from the following list to complete the statements below.

interdependence   diplomatic recognition
alliance   diplomatic corps
executive agreement   couriers

1. U.S. ambassadors, ministers, and consuls are members of the

_____.

2. _____ may also be referred to as mutual reliance.

3. _____ means that the president may decide whether to recognize the government of a foreign country.

4. _____ are special messengers who transport important reports.

5. A(n) _____ is an agreement between countries to help each other for defense, economic, scientific, or other reasons.

6. The president and the leader of a foreign government may meet and establish a

mutual understanding, or _____.

Foreign Policy

VOCABULARY Some terms to understand:

• **conducting (p. 581):** guiding or managing

• **aggression (p. 582):** violence or hostility

• **devastation (p. 582):** destruction

• **restrictions (p. 585):** limits

• **vehicles (p. 586):** tools

REVIEWING FACTS Choose the correct terms from the following list to complete the statements below.

summit	exports	free trade
foreign aid	imports	newly industrialized countries
balance of trade	trade deficits	

1. _____ refers to any government program that provides economic or military assistance to another country.

2. _____ is trade that is not restricted by tariffs and other trade barriers.

3. The _____ is the difference in the value between a country's exports and imports over a period of time.

4. _____ are those goods and services that the United States sells to other countries.

5. A(n) _____ is a meeting between the leaders of two or more countries to discuss issues that concern those countries.

6. _____ have experienced rapid industrialization and economic growth in recent years.

7. _____ are those goods and services that the United States buys from other countries.

8. _____ occur when the country spends more money buying imports than it earns from selling exports to other countries.

Chapter 23, Main Idea Activities 23.2, continued

EVALUATING INFORMATION Mark each statement *T* if it is true or *F* if it is false.

_____ **1.** The United States refused to sign the North American Free-Trade Agreement (NAFTA).

_____ **2.** The United States does not have an alliance with Japan or South Korea.

_____ **3.** The United States gave large amounts of foreign aid during World War II.

_____ **4.** In recent decades, foreign competition and economic alliances in other parts of the world have challenged the economic position of the United States.

_____ **5.** The European Union was formed in 1930.

_____ **6.** Opponents of free trade believe that tariffs are needed to protect American industries and jobs from foreign competition.

_____ **7.** Environmental policy has no influence on foreign relations.

_____ **8.** The president is the chief diplomat of the United States.

UNDERSTANDING MAIN IDEAS For each of the following, write the letter of the best choice in the space provided.

_____ **1.** The name of the organization established in 1949 to form a united front against communism is known as
   a. OAS.
   b. APEC.
   c. NATO.
   d. NAFTA.

_____ **2.** The name of the organization that promotes cooperation among Asia-Pacific countries is known as
   a. OAS.
   b. APEC.
   c. NATO.
   d. NAFTA.

_____ **3.** The name of the organization that formed an alliance between Australia, New Zealand, and the United States is
   a. OAS.
   b. NATO.
   c. ANZUS.
   d. WTO.

_____ **4.** Which of the following is an example of an NIC?
   a. the United States
   b. France
   c. Australia
   d. South Korea

Name _____ Class _____ Date _____

 Main Idea Activities 23.3

Foreign Policy

VOCABULARY Some terms to understand:

- **principles (p. 588):** main beliefs or values
- **equipped (p. 591):** prepared or ready
- **authorized (p. 592):** allowed
- **stabilize (p. 592):** to even out or become constant
- **forum (p. 592):** environment

ORGANIZING INFORMATION Fill in the chart below to illustrate the names and jobs of each of the divisions of the United Nations.

NAME OF DIVISION	WHAT DIVISION DOES

Chapter 23, Main Idea Activities 23.3, continued

REVIEWING FACTS Choose the correct terms from the following list to complete the statements below.

United Nations   Security Council
General Assembly   International Court of Justice

1. The _____ is also known as the World Court.

2. The sessions of the _____ begin on the third Tuesday in September.

3. The _____ has five permanent members including China, France, and the United States.

4. The _____ was formed to promote peaceful coexistence and worldwide cooperation.

EVALUATING INFORMATION Mark each statement *T* if it is true or *F* if it is false.

_____ **1.** The General Assembly elects representatives from 54 countries to serve as members of the Economic and Social Council.

_____ **2.** The Secretariat has nearly 9,000 staff members.

_____ **3.** The United Nations has six main divisions.

_____ **4.** The World Health Organization extends educational opportunities everywhere in the world.

_____ **5.** UN peacekeepers are authorized to use force in settling disputes only in extremely dangerous situations.

_____ **6.** The Atlantic Charter dictated that no country should try to gain territory as a result of war.

_____ **7.** All important issues must be agreed on by a two-thirds majority in the General Assembly.

_____ **8.** The Security Council includes one member from every country involved in the UN.

Name ______________________ Class ____________ Date ____________

CHAPTER 24 Main Idea Activities 24.1

Charting a Course

VOCABULARY Some terms to understand:

- **ventured (p. 598):** risked or tried
- **internal (p. 600):** happening inside or within a country
- **intervention (p. 600):** involvement or interference

ORGANIZING INFORMATION Fill in the chart below to illustrate the conflicts between the United States and other countries, and the ultimate results.

UNITED STATES AND:	CONFLICT	RESULT
CANADA		
LATIN AMERICA		
GERMANY		
JAPAN		

Chapter 24, Main Idea Activities 24.1, continued

EVALUATING INFORMATION Mark each statement *T* if it is true or *F* if it is false.

_____ **1.** When the United States won its independence, most government leaders believed in isolationism.

_____ **2.** The War of 1812 ended in a stalemate.

_____ **3.** The Rush-Bagot Agreement was the first step in creating hostility between the United States and Canada that still continues today.

_____ **4.** At first, Latin America appreciated the Monroe Doctrine.

_____ **5.** The United States sent troops to Latin America only when conflict within Latin America threatened U.S. investments.

_____ **6.** The United States stayed neutral throughout World Wars I and II.

_____ **7.** Many Senators opposed U.S. membership in the League of Nations.

_____ **8.** The Japanese bombed Pearl Harbor on December 7, 1941.

_____ **9.** In 1812, Americans claimed that Britain was arming American Indians on the western borders of the United States.

_____ **10.** President Abraham Lincoln created the Monroe Doctrine.

REVIEWING FACTS Choose the correct items from the following list to complete the statements below.

isolationism   dollar diplomacy
doctrine   neutrality
corollary

1. A(n) _____ sets forth a new way of interacting with other countries.

2. A(n) _____ is a statement that follows as a natural or logical result.

3. _____ dictates that the United States should avoid involvement in all foreign affairs.

4. If a country adopts a policy of _____, then it does not assist or favor either side in a disagreement.

5. U.S. foreign policy in Latin America became known as _____ when the United States sent troops to maintain peace only when its investments were threatened.

Name _____ Class _____ Date _____

 Main Idea Activities 24.2

Charting a Course

VOCABULARY Some terms to understand:

• **guerillas (p. 612):** rebels

• **heated (p. 612):** intense

REVIEWING FACTS Choose the correct items from the following list to complete the statements below.

communism	balance of power	perestroika
satellite nations	limited war	détente
containment	glasnost	

1. A situation in which countries are about equal in strength is called a

_____.

2. _____ is an economic system in which the working class takes over factories and businesses, thereby preventing any group from owning all the means of production.

3. The purpose of _____ was to prevent Soviet communism from spreading to other countries.

4. A _____ is fought without using a country's full power, particularly nuclear weapons.

5. Gorbachev introduced a policy called _____, or openness, aimed at giving the Soviet people more freedom.

6. _____ are those countries that are controlled by another country.

7. _____ means restructuring.

8. _____ means the lessening of tensions.

EVALUATING INFORMATION Mark each statement *T* if it is true or *F* if it is false.

_____ **1.** Karl Marx and Friedrich Engels proposed communism.

_____ **2.** In 1917 China became the first country to adopt a communist system.

_____ **3.** The Soviet Union and the United States had been enemies during World War II.

_____ **4.** When Harry Truman warned the Soviet Union to withdraw its troops from Iran, they refused.

_____ **5.** In 1949, Chinese communists overthrew Chiang Kaishek and Mao Zedong came to power.

_____ **6.** Fidel Castro set up a communist government in Cuba in 1959.

_____ **7.** Currently, North Korea is communist and South Korea is not.

_____ **8.** The northern communist government eventually controlled all of Vietnam.

_____ **9.** The Cold War is still a major problem.

_____ **10.** During the Cuban missile crisis, the United States refused to deliver weapons to Cuba.

UNDERSTANDING MAIN IDEAS For each of the following, write the letter of the best choice in the space provided.

_____ **1.** Which of the following countries is or was at one time communist?
   a. Cuba
   b. the United States
   c. Canada
   d. France

_____ **2.** One belief of communism is that
   a. the proletariat own businesses.
   b. private individuals own land.
   c. raw materials are owned by citizens.
   d. it is only a political, not an economic, system.

_____ **3.** All of the following countries occupied the western zone in Germany after World War II EXCEPT
   a. the United States.
   b. the Soviet Union.
   c. France.
   d. Great Britain.

_____ **4.** During the Cuban missile crisis, the United States
   a. delivered weapons to Cuba.
   b. accompanied and protected foreign ships bound for Cuba.
   c. put army troops on alert.
   d. all of the above.

Main Idea Activities 24.3

Charting a Course

VOCABULARY Some terms to understand:

• **assault (p. 615):** physical attack

• **condemned (p. 617):** declared to be wrong

• **earmarked (p. 617):** set aside for

• **vital (p. 618):** very important

CLASSIFYING INFORMATION For each of the following, write the letter of the correct choice in the space provided.

_____ **1.** There is great tension between this country and the Palestinians.

_____ **2.** This country invaded Kuwait in 1990.

_____ **3.** For decades, this country operated under apartheid.

_____ **4.** The United States recently withdrew from the Anti-ballistic Missile Treaty signed by this country.

_____ **5.** Nelson Mandela was president of this country.

_____ **6.** Saddam Hussein was removed as leader of this country.

_____ **7.** Seventy percent of adults who have HIV live in this country.

_____ **8.** The United States fought this country during the Gulf War.

_____ **9.** In 1995, this country joined NATO's Partnership for Peace program.

_____ **10.** This nation was created in 1948.

a. Russia

b. Iraq

c. Israel

d. South Africa

Chapter 24, Main Idea Activities 24.3, continued

EVALUATING INFORMATION Mark each statement *T* if it is true or *F* if it is false.

_____ 1. India and Pakistan have fought three wars since the two countries won their independence from Great Britain.

_____ 2. The People's Republic of China is no longer communist.

_____ 3. Cuba is the only communist country in Latin America.

_____ 4. President George W. Bush created the Office of Homeland Security after the terrorist attacks of September 11, 2001.

_____ 5. One of the U.S. government's goals in its fight against terrorism was to isolate the Taliban regime.

_____ 6. Countries such as Great Britain and Russia have refused to support the antiterrorist efforts of the United States.

_____ 7. The U.S. government has given money toward AIDS prevention and care in Africa.

_____ 8. The main goal of U.S. foreign policy in Latin America today is to expand trade and open new markets.

_____ 9. The War on Drugs began in the 1950s.

_____ 10. An embargo, or government order against trade between the United States and Cuba, is no longer in effect.

_____ 11. In the fight against terrorism, President Bush emphasized that U.S. efforts would be aimed not only against terrorist organizations but also against national governments that supported terrorism.

_____ 12. Foreign policies rarely change.

CHAPTER **25**

Main Idea Activities 25.1

Improving Life for All Americans

VOCABULARY Some terms to understand:

- **inefficient (p. 627):** wasteful
- **relocated (p. 628):** moved
- **revitalize (p. 629):** to renew or revive
- **restore (p. 629):** to bring back or repair
- **decline (p. 632):** decrease

ORGANIZING INFORMATION Fill in the diagram below to illustrate the structure of a city and its surrounding areas.

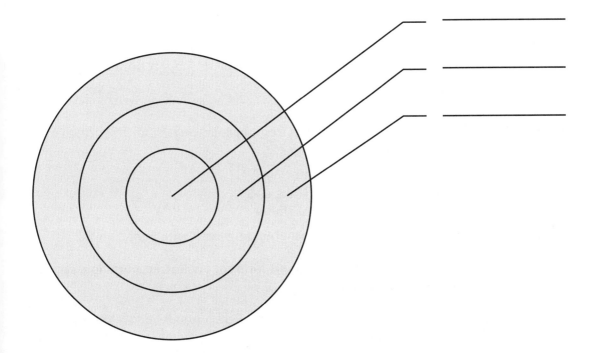

Chapter 25, Main Idea Activities 25.1, continued

EVALUATING INFORMATION Mark each statement *T* if it is true or *F* if it is false.

_____ **1.** Since urban areas were created, the quality of life in these areas has improved.

_____ **2.** Many homeless people are unable to get jobs because they have no permanent address and phone number.

_____ **3.** The federal government has not helped to solve the problem of homelessness.

_____ **4.** Through the years, more and more people have started using mass transit.

_____ **5.** Many cities and suburbs have formed metropolitan transit authorities.

_____ **6.** Typically, cities today are divided into two parts—the older, central part of the city and the suburbs.

_____ **7.** During the mid- to late 1900s, the centers of American cities began losing population.

_____ **8.** Urban-renewal programs usually receive financial support from the federal government.

REVIEWING FACTS Choose the correct items from the following list to complete the statements below.

public housing projects   zoning laws
urban-renewal programs   building codes
homelessness   mass transit

1. _____ are apartment buildings built with public funds.

2. _____ includes various forms of public transportation, such as subways, buses, and commuter railroads.

3. _____ improve neglected neighborhoods and restore and maintain buildings in a particular area.

4. _____ regulate the kinds of buildings and businesses that may be located in a certain area.

5. _____ is a major social problem that affects 750,000 people today.

6. _____ dictate that buildings be inspected regularly.

CHAPTER **25**   Main Idea Activities 25.2

Improving Life for All Americans

VOCABULARY Some terms to understand:

- **heritage (p. 634):** tradition
- **exploited (p. 635):** took advantage of
- **denied (p. 635):** did not allow
- **convicted (p. 637):** found guilty

ORGANIZING INFORMATION Fill in the diagram below with the names of minority groups in the United States.

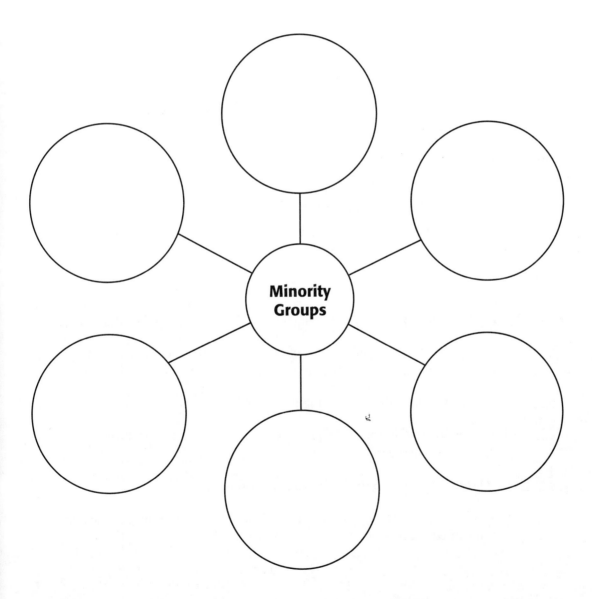

REVIEWING FACTS Choose the correct items from the following list to complete the statements below.

minority groups	civil rights movement	demonstration
discrimination	boycott	civil disobedience
ethnic group	dissent	

1. People who supported the _____ opposed laws that denied equal rights to African Americans and others.

2. A(n) _____ consists of people of the same race, nationality, or religion who share a common, distinctive culture and heritage.

3. _____ do not have as much political or economic power as other groups.

4. _____ refers to unfair actions taken against people because they belong to a particular group.

5. A(n) _____ calls for people to stop using a particular product or service.

6. During a(n) _____, dissenters march in public carrying signs, singing songs, and making speeches.

7. Intentionally disobeying laws that you believe are wrong is called

_____.

8. _____ means disagreement.

EVALUATING INFORMATION Mark each statement *T* if it is true or *F* if it is false.

_____ 1. Older citizens, with their wealth of experience, are particularly able to make valuable contributions to society.

_____ 2. Martin Luther King Jr. was a major leader in the civil rights movement.

_____ 3. People involved in the civil rights movement used one basic means of fighting for change.

_____ 4. Discrimination in public schools is against the law.

_____ 5. Hispanics form one of the smallest and slowest-growing minority groups in the United States.

Main Idea Activities 25.3

Improving Life for All Americans

VOCABULARY Some terms to understand:

- **welfare (p. 644):** well-being
- **skyrocket (p. 645):** to increase quickly or drastically
- **recreation (p. 646):** leisure or pastime
- **impairs (p. 646):** weakens
- **compulsive (p. 646):** uncontrollable
- **strain (p. 647):** to injure or damage
- **exceed (p. 649):** to go beyond
- **hazards (p. 650):** dangers
- **detects (p. 650):** identifies or perceives

ORGANIZING INFORMATION Fill in the chart below with the dangers to people's health that were discussed in the text and list ways to prevent the damage they cause.

DANGERS	PREVENTATIVE MEASURES

Chapter 25, Main Idea Activities 25.3, *continued*

EVALUATING INFORMATION Mark each statement *T* if it is true or *F* if it is false.

_____ **1.** The federal government spends billions of dollars each year on health programs.

_____ **2.** Each state's department of public health sees that health laws are enforced in every part of the state.

_____ **3.** Drugs prescribed by physicians are harmless.

_____ **4.** The quality of drugs sold illegally by drug dealers is regulated.

_____ **5.** Alcohol is a factor in nearly half of all fatal automobile accidents.

_____ **6.** Smoking poses a threat to smokers but not to nonsmokers.

_____ **7.** A federal law requires that all cigarette packages and advertisements carry a warning about the dangers of smoking.

_____ **8.** HIV destroys a body's immune system, thereby making people who suffer from it more likely to contract diseases.

_____ **9.** People who contract AIDS become sick immediately.

_____ **10.** The AIDS virus is transmitted through casual contact such as shaking hands.

_____ **11.** In recent years, AIDS appears to be spreading faster among heterosexuals than among any other group.

_____ **12.** Many accidents happen in the home or on the job.

_____ **13.** If everyone wore a seatbelt, thousands of lives would be saved each year.

_____ **14.** Smoke detectors are not effective in warning of a fire in the home.

Main Idea Activities 26.1

The Global Environment

VOCABULARY Some terms to understand:

- **interdependent (p. 655):** relying on one another
- **vital (p. 655):** very important
- **hides (p. 657):** animal skins
- **extinct (p. 658):** wiped out or dead
- **tolerance (p. 660):** open-mindedness

ORGANIZING INFORMATION Place the life forms in their appropriate place in the food chain.

fish   humans
shrimp   plankton

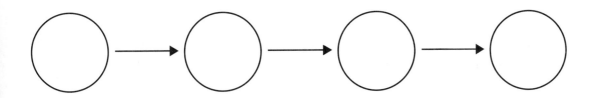

Chapter 26, Main Idea Activities 26.1, continued

EVALUATING INFORMATION Mark each statement *T* if it is true or *F* if it is false.

_____ **1.** Forests provide protection and food for many animals.

_____ **2.** Early settlers did not have enough trees and forests for their needs.

_____ **3.** Early settlers killed animals for food only and used every part of the animal.

_____ **4.** As the land was farmed year after year, it became more fertile.

_____ **5.** All farmers have stopped using fertilizers and pesticides.

_____ **6.** Overpopulation strains the world's natural resources.

_____ **7.** In general, food production can keep up with population growth.

_____ **8.** All living things depend on each other for survival.

REVIEWING FACTS Choose the correct items from the following list to complete the statements below.

ecology	desertification	organic farming
ecosystem	fertilizers	
erosion	pesticides	

1. _____ is defined as the wearing away of land by water and wind.

2. _____ does not include the use of artificial substances.

3. A(n) _____ is a community of interdependent living things existing in balance with their physical environment.

4. _____ is a process that occurs when years of overgrazing and removal of plants harm the soil, and once-fertile areas become deserts.

5. _____ are plant foods that make crops grow faster and bigger.

6. The study of living things in relation to each other and their environment is called

_____.

7. _____ are chemicals that kill insect pests and weeds.

VOCABULARY Some terms to understand:

- **precious (p. 662):** valuable
- **habitable (p. 664):** able to support life
- **devastating (p. 664):** destructive
- **discard (p. 666):** to throw away
- **deposited (p. 667):** put down, left
- **decompose (p. 667):** to rot or decay

ORGANIZING INFORMATION Fill in the chart below with types of pollution and how each may be prevented.

TYPE OF POLLUTION	PREVENTATIVE MEASURES

Chapter 26, Main Idea Activities 26.2, continued

REVIEWING FACTS Choose the correct items from the following list to complete the statements below.

pollution	greenhouse effect	hydrologic cycle
renewable resource	ozone layer	landfills
smog	acid rain	recycling

1. _____ occurs when pollution from burning gas, oil, and coal mixes with water vapor to form acid.

2. _____ is the process of turning waste into something that can be used again.

3. _____ results when any part of the environment becomes contaminated, or unfit for use.

4. A(n) _____, such as the air we breath, can be replaced.

5. _____ are huge pits dug in the ground and used to store large amounts of garbage.

6. The _____ explains how water recycles itself.

7. A combination of smoke, gases, and fog is called _____.

8. The process in which an increase in carbon dioxide in the atmosphere raises the

Earth's temperature is called the _____.

9. The _____ is a thin layer in the upper atmosphere that shields the Earth from the Sun's ultraviolet rays.

UNDERSTANDING MAIN IDEAS For each of the following, write the letter of the best choice in the space provided.

_____ 1. All of the following are steps in the hydrologic cycle EXCEPT
   a. Water evaporates into the atmosphere.
   b. Rain sinks into the soil.
   c. Excess water runs into lakes, rivers, and oceans.
   d. Humans treat sewage so it can be used as drinking water.

_____ 2. Which of the following is one type of water pollution?
   a. chemical
   b. poison
   c. smog
   d. all of the above

The Global Environment

VOCABULARY Some terms to understand:

- **reserves (p. 671):** something stored away
- **reliance (p. 672):** dependence
- **consumption (p. 672):** use
- **debris (p. 672):** fragments
- **compressed (p. 672):** packed in
- **synthetic (p. 673):** artificial or fake
- **prone (p. 673):** likely
- **mutations (p. 674):** changes or differences
- **dispose (p. 674):** to get rid of
- **generate (p. 675):** to produce

ORGANIZING INFORMATION Fill in the chart below with renewable and nonrenewable resources.

RENEWABLE RESOURCES	NONRENEWABLE RESOURCES

Chapter 26, Main Idea Activities 26.3, continued

EVALUATING INFORMATION Mark each statement *T* if it is true or *F* if it is false.

_____ **1.** Coal is the most plentiful fossil fuel, and it is even renewable.

_____ **2.** The explosion at Chernobyl affected only the people who were in the plant at the time.

_____ **3.** Solar energy is a very promising source of alternative energy.

_____ **4.** Biomass consists of wood and waste products such as garbage and yard trimmings.

_____ **5.** Petroleum is the basis of a wide variety of by-products, such as plastics, pesticides, and many chemicals.

_____ **6.** The world's supply of oil is unlimited.

_____ **7.** Home owners are not able to do anything to conserve oil.

_____ **8.** Most of the energy contained in natural gas is used to generate steam for electricity and steam engines.

_____ **9.** Natural gas is the cleanest-burning fossil fuel.

_____ **10.** Worldwide demand for natural gas has increased greatly in recent years.

_____ **11.** Strip mining is an effective and harmless way of getting coal.

_____ **12.** Burning coal can result in air pollution and acid rain.

_____ **13.** Most people support the use of nuclear energy.

_____ **14.** Geothermal energy is also known as underground heat.

Main Idea Activities 26.4

The Global Environment

VOCABULARY Some terms to understand:

- **vast (p. 677):** very large
- **grazing (p. 677):** eating plants as they grow
- **irrigate (p. 678):** to water
- **refuse (p. 678):** garbage or waste
- **provisions (p. 680):** requirements

ORGANIZING INFORMATION Fill in the diagram below with some of the laws that the U.S. government has passed to reduce pollution and restore the environment.

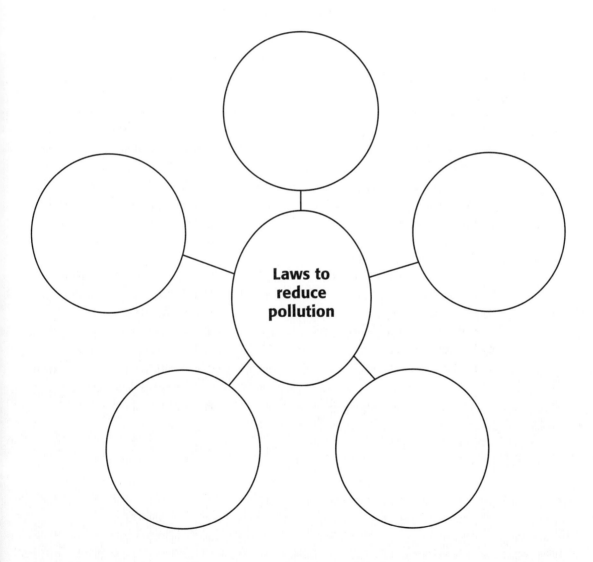

Laws to reduce pollution

Chapter 26, Main Idea Activities 26.4, continued

EVALUATING INFORMATION Mark each statement *T* if it is true or *F* if it is false.

_____ **1.** The National Park Service is the only agency that helps preserve the natural resources of the United States.

_____ **2.** The head of the Environmental Protection Agency (EPA) reports directly to the president.

_____ **3.** Earth Day is an unofficial holiday dedicated to caring for the Earth.

_____ **4.** Federal, state, and local laws cannot guarantee that the environment will be protected.

_____ **5.** Yellowstone National Park was the first national park in the world.

_____ **6.** President John F. Kennedy was the first president who cared about the environment.

UNDERSTANDING MAIN IDEAS For each of the following, write the letter of the best choice in the space provided.

_____ **1.** Which of the following laws helps to reduce air pollution?
   a. Clean Air Acts
   b. water pollution control acts
   c. Wilderness Act
   d. Endangered Species Acts

_____ **2.** Which of the following laws helped to save the American bald eagle?
   a. Clean Air Acts
   b. water pollution control acts
   c. Wilderness Act
   d. Endangered Species Acts

_____ **3.** Which of the following laws designated areas of land to be kept in their natural state?
   a. Clean Air Acts
   b. water pollution control acts
   c. Wilderness Act
   d. Endangered Species Acts

_____ **4.** Which of the following can you do to help protect the environment?
   a. Do not waste food.
   b. Recycle.
   c. Do not destroy wildlife or damage public resources.
   d. all of the above

Chapter 1

SECTION 1
Organizing Information

Roles: vote in elections; inform officials of your needs and disagreements with government; study civics

Qualities: answers may vary (examples: are responsible family members; respect and obey the laws of the land; take an active part in government)

Evaluating Information

1. F	6. T
2. T	7. T
3. T	8. F
4. F	9. T
5. T	10. F

Reviewing Facts

1. resources
2. Government
3. heritage
4. civics
5. citizen

SECTION 2
Evaluating Information

1. F	6. T
2. F	7. F
3. T	8. F
4. T	9. T
5. T	

Reviewing Facts

1. Aliens
2. naturalization
3. quotas
4. refugees
5. immigrant
6. native-born citizen
7. deport

Understanding Main Ideas

1. a
2. d

SECTION 3
Orgainizing Information

Population—increase; number of people in rural areas—decrease; number of people living in suburbs—increase; migration—increase; diversity of population—increase; size of household—decrease; age of population—increase.

Evaluating Information

1. T	5. T
2. F	6. F
3. T	7. T
4. F	8. T

Reviewing Facts

1. birthrate
2. migration
3. census
4. Death rate
5. suburb
6. rural area
7. Sunbelt

Chapter 2

SECTION 1
Organizing Information

1. It helps people cooperate by enabling them to work together as a group easily and safely. Example: people can better protect themselves against enemies when united—armies.
2. It provides services which may not be accomplished individually. Example: education.
3. It provides rules through laws. Example: keep your sidewalk in good shape and others do the same.
4. It puts our ideals into practice. Example: safeguards our rights.

Evaluating Information

1. F	4. T
2. F	5. T
3. T	

Reviewing Facts

1. dictatorship
2. representative democracy
3. monarchies
4. totalitarian
5. democracy
6. authoritarian
7. direct democracy
8. laws
9. republic
10. constitution

SECTION 2
Organizing Information

The government was powerless in ending states' disputes over trade and the location of boundary lines. Unable to collect taxes, Congress could not pay the country's debts or carry on any needed government activities. There was no guarantee that the laws passed by Congress would be carried out. There was little contact between the states. The states did not see themselves as parts of a whole country. A national currency did not exist.

Evaluating Information

1. T	5. F
2. T	6. T
3. F	7. F
4. F	8. T

Understanding Main Ideas

1. c
2. b
3. b
4. a
5. c

SECTION 3
Reviewing Facts

1. ratification
2. Federalists
3. delegates
4. Parliament
5. compromise
6. unitary system
7. bicameral
8. Federalism
9. legislature
10. Antifederalists

Evaluating Information

1. T	7. F
2. F	8. F
3. T	9. T
4. F	10. T
5. T	11. F
6. T	12. T

Chapter 3

SECTION 1
Organizing Information

Powers of federal government—coins money, controls trade with foreign nations, provides for country's defense

Powers of state government—conducts elections, regulates trade within states, establishes local governments

Overlapping powers—raise funds through taxes, borrow money, establish courts, charter banks, enforce laws, punish lawbreakers, provide for health and welfare of citizens

Evaluating Information

1. T	4. F
2. F	5. T
3. F	6. T

Reviewing Facts

1. limited government
2. reserved power
3. delegated powers
4. Popular sovereignty
5. Preamble
6. majority rule
7. concurrent powers

SECTION 2
Organizing Information

Legislative—makes laws. (Circles below should read "Senate" and "House of Representatives.")
Executive—carries out laws.
Judicial—interprets laws and punishes lawbreakers.

Evaluating Information

1. F	4. T
2. F	5. T
3. T	

Understanding Main Ideas

1. b   4. c
2. a   5. d
3. b   6. b

SECTION 3
Organizing Information

Step 1: Propose amendment—Option #1: Two thirds vote in both houses. Option #2: Two thirds of states ask Congress to hold national convention.
Step 2: Ratify amendment—Option #1: State legislatures approve. Option #2: State conventions approve.

Evaluating Information

1. F   7. T
2. T   8. F
3. T   9. T
4. F   10. T
5. T   11. T
6. F   12. F

Chapter 4

SECTION 1
Classifying Information

1. Fourth Amendment
2. Second Amendment
3. Sixth Amendment
4. First Amendment

Evaluating Information

1. F   5. T
2. T   6. T
3. F   7. T
4. T   8. F

Reviewing Facts

1. separation of church and state
2. search warrant
3. eminent domain
4. slander
5. libel
6. indicted

SECTION 2
Organizing Information

1. outlawed slavery
2. granted citizenship to African Americans, all citizens have equal protection under the law
3. Fifteenth
4. Seventeenth
5. granted women the right to vote
6. granted people of Washington, D.C., the right to vote
7. Twenty-fourth
8. lowered voting age from 21 to 18

Evaluating Information

1. F   5. T
2. F   6. F
3. T   7. T
4. T

Understanding Main Ideas

1. c   5. c
2. a   6. b
3. c   7. a
4. a   8. a

SECTION 3
Classifying Information

1. attending school
2. paying taxes
3. obeying the law
4. appearing in court
5. serving in the armed forces

Evaluating Information

1. T   6. F
2. F   7. T
3. T   8. T
4. F   9. F
5. F   10. T

Reviewing Facts

1. Taxes
2. draft
3. duties

Chapter 5

SECTION 1
Organizing Information

House of Representatives—members: 435; terms: two years; qualifications: must be at least 25, have been a U.S. citizen for at least seven years, be a legal resident of the state he or she represents.
Senate—members: 100; terms: six years; qualifications: must be at least 30, have been a U.S. citizen for at least nine years, be a legal resident of the state he or she represents.

Evaluating Information

1. T	**5.** F
2. F	**6.** T
3. T	**7.** F
4. T	**8.** F

Reviewing Facts

1. franking privilege
2. expulsion
3. apportioned
4. immunity
5. gerrymandering

SECTION 2
Organizing Information

House of Representatives—clockwise from top: Speaker of the House, majority leader, majority party, minority party, minority leader.

Senate—clockwise: Vice President, president *pro tempore*, majority leader, majority party, minority party, minority leader.

Evaluating Information

1. T	**4.** F
2. T	**5.** F
3. F	**6.** T

Understanding Main Ideas

1. c	**3.** b
2. a	**4.** d

SECTION 3
Reviewing Facts

1. writ of *habeas corpus*
2. elastic clause
3. impeached
4. implied powers
5. bill of attainder
6. constituents
7. treason
8. *ex post facto* law

Evaluating Information

1. F	**8.** T
2. F	**9.** F
3. T	**10.** T
4. T	**11.** T
5. F	**12.** F
6. F	**13.** T
7. F	**14.** F

SECTION 4
Organizing Information

Congressmembers have idea for a bill. Bill is written out. Bill is printed in *Congressional Record*. Bill is sent to standing committee. Bill is revised. House passes bill. Senate passes bill. President approves bill.

Evaluating Information

1. F	**5.** F
2. T	**6.** T
3. T	**7.** F
4. T	**8.** T

Reviewing Facts

1. filibuster
2. appropriation bill
3. quorum
4. role-call vote
5. cloture

Chapter 6

SECTION 1
Organizing Information

vice president; Speaker of the House; president *pro tempore* of Senate; members of president's cabinet in the order in which the departments were created.

Evaluating Information

1. T	**7.** T
2. F	**8.** T
3. T	**9.** F
4. F	**10.** F
5. F	**11.** F
6. T	**12.** T

Reviewing Facts

1. presidential succession
2. two
3. Camp David
4. men
5. Speaker of the House

SECTION 2
Evaluating Information

1. T	**6.** T
2. F	**7.** T
3. F	**8.** F
4. T	**9.** F
5. F	**10.** T

Reviewing Facts

1. diplomatic notes
2. pardon
3. treaties
4. foreign policy
5. reprieve

Understanding Main Ideas

1. d
2. a
3. c

SECTION 3
Reviewing Facts

1. embassy
2. consul
3. budget
4. attorney general
5. executive departments
6. secretary
7. counterfeiting
8. Ambassadors
9. ministers
10. Visas
11. Passports
12. civilian

Evaluating Information

1. T
2. F
3. T
4. F
5. T
6. F
7. T
8. F
9. T
10. T

SECTION 4
Organizing Information

Independent agencies—purpose: perform specific job; examples and what they do: answers may vary.

Regulatory commissions—purpose: independent agencies that make rules and bring violators to court; examples and what they do: answers may vary.

Federal bureaucracy—purpose: perform day-to-day work of the executive branch; examples and what they do: answers may vary.

Evaluating Information

1. T
2. F
3. T
4. T
5. F
6. T
7. T
8. F
9. T
10. F
11. T
12. F

Reviewing Facts

1. Consumer Product Safety Commission
2. regulatory commission
3. National Labor Relations Board
4. independent agency
5. Office of Personnel Management

Chapter 7

SECTION 1
Organizing Information

Statutory law—laws passed by Congress and state and local governments. Example: State law requires fire exits in all public buildings.
Common law—rule based on common sense. Example: If there is no law for speed limit, apply law that states people cannot use property to injure others.
Administrative law—laws created by government agencies. Example: Unsafe toy must be recalled.
Constitutional law—law based on the Constitution. Example: freedom of speech.

Evaluating Information

1. T
2. F
3. T
4. F
5. F
6. F
7. T
8. T
9. F
10. T

Reviewing Facts

1. appeal
2. hung jury
3. precedent
4. testimony
5. petit jury
6. Jurors
7. common
8. verdict
9. cross-examine

SECTION 2

Reviewing Facts

1. court-martial
2. marshal
3. original
4. circuit
5. Jurisdiction
6. Territorial courts
7. subpoena
8. courts of appeals

Evaluating Information

1. T	5. F
2. T	6. T
3. T	7. T
4. F	8. T

Understanding Main Ideas

1. d	3. b
2. b	4. a

SECTION 3

Organizing Information

(1) Justices agree to hear a particular case.
(2) Justices study briefs prepared by lawyers.
(3) Lawyers for each side present oral arguments. (4) Justices question lawyers. (5) Justice writes opinion of the court.

Evaluating Information

1. T	8. T
2. F	9. F
3. T	10. T
4. T	11. F
5. F	12. F
6. F	13. F
7. T	14. F

Chapter 8

SECTION 1

Organizing Information

Federal government—regulate trade between states, coin money, conduct foreign affairs, set up a postal service, maintain an army and navy. Concurrent powers—establish court systems, borrow and spend money, make and enforce laws. State government—conduct elections, make laws concerning education, marriage and divorce, health, highway traffic, safety, and welfare, regulate business, and grant powers to local government.

Evaluating Information

1. T	7. F
2. T	8. T
3. F	9. T
4. T	10. T
5. F	
6. F	

Reviewing Facts

1. extradition
2. concurrent powers
3. full faith and credit clause
4. territories

SECTION 2

Organizing Information

Initiative—Citizens draw up a petition describing the proposal. If enough voters sign the petition, the proposition appears on the ballot in the next general election. Referendum—when some bills passed by legislature must be approved by voters; questions are asked directly to the citizens. Recall—Required number of voters sign a petition to remove an elected official from office.

Evaluating Information

1. F	5. F
2. T	6. T
3. F	7. T
4. T	8. T

Understanding Main Ideas

1. a	3. c
2. c	4. d

SECTION 3

Organizing Information

Governor urges state legislatures as to which bills to pass and which to oppose. He or she puts laws into force. He or she draws up a budget for the state. He or she may order the state militia to do something. He or she may pardon a prisoner.

Evaluating Information

1. T	5. F
2. F	6. F
3. T	7. T
4. F	8. F

Reviewing Facts

1. warrant
2. governor
3. patronage
4. lieutenant governor
5. executive orders

SECTION 4
Organizing Information

Lower Courts—hear minor cases such as misdemeanors and civil cases involving small amounts of money. General trial courts—hear major criminal and civil cases. Appeals courts—hear cases in which a person believes his or her case was not handled fairly in a trial court. State supreme court—highest court in most states, hear appeal cases.

Reviewing Facts

1. plaintiff
2. general trial courts
3. civil cases
4. justice of the peace
5. penal code
6. small claims court
7. complaint
8. criminal cases
9. municipal courts

Classifying Information

1. a
2. b
3. a
4. d
5. c
6. b

Chapter 9
SECTION 1

Organizing Information

Sheriff—enforces law and selects deputies. County clerk—keeps a record of actions and decisions of the county board, as well as records of births, deaths, marriages, and election results.
Treasurer—takes care of the county's funds.
Auditor—examines official records of taxes and money spent to ensure they are kept properly.
District attorney—represents the state government in county trials.

Evaluating Information

1. T
2. T
3. F
4. F
5. F
6. T
7. F
8. F

Reviewing Facts

1. ordinance
2. county clerk
3. charters
4. county seat
5. sheriff
6. municipality
7. district attorney
8. counties

SECTION 2
Organizing Information

Towns—Definition: land including settlers' homes, churches, and farms. Government: issues decided at town meetings.
Townships—Definition: counties divided into these smaller units of local government. Government: municipal and county governments hold more importance now; voters elect board of commissioners.
Villages—Definition: land that included only the homes and buildings of settlers, not their farms. Government: a self-governing municipality, governed by a small council.

Evaluating Information

1. T
2. F
3. T
4. T
5. T
6. F
7. T
8. F
9. T
10. T
11. F
12. T

Understanding Main Ideas

1. c
2. b
3. c
4. a

SECTION 3
Classifying Information

1. b
2. c
3. a
4. d
5. b
6. d
7. a
8. d
9. a
10. c
11. d
12. b

Evaluating Information

1. F
2. T
3. F
4. T
5. T
6. F
7. F
8. T

Reviewing Facts
1. home rule
2. council members at large
3. City council
4. wards
5. city
6. commission

SECTION 4
Organizing Information
Road building, education, law enforcement, business practices, licensing boards, grants-in-aid.

Evaluating Information
1. F	**7.** F
2. T	**8.** T
3. T	**9.** T
4. F	**10.** T
5. F	**11.** T
6. F	**12.** F

Chapter 10
SECTION 1
Organizing Information
First political parties—Federalists; Antifederalists. Political parties in the 1820s–today—Democrats; Republicans. Examples of third parties—Progressive Party; American Independent Party; Populist Party.

Evaluating Information
1. F	**6.** F
2. F	**7.** T
3. T	**8.** T
4. T	**9.** T
5. T	**10.** F

Reviewing Facts
1. nominate
2. one-party system
3. coalition
4. political party
5. two-party system
6. third party
7. Candidates
8. multiparty system

SECTION 2
Organizing Information
National committee—members elected by state convention, by voters in statewide election, or chosen by state central committee; selects city in which national nominating convention will be held; publishes and distributes party literature; arranges for campaign speakers; helps to raise money for campaign. State central committees—chairperson one of party's most prominent members in the state; maintains party harmony and raises money for campaigns.

Local committees—members elected by party members; conducts campaigns on local level and raises money for party candidate.

Evaluating Information
1. F	**4.** T
2. F	**5.** T
3. T	

Understanding Main Ideas
1. d	**3.** b
2. c	**4.** c

SECTION 3
Evaluating Information
1. F	**8.** F
2. F	**9.** F
3. T	**10.** T
4. F	**11.** F
5. T	**12.** T
6. T	**13.** F
7. T	**14.** T

Reviewing Facts
1. closed primary
2. grassroots support
3. primary election
4. general election
5. runoff
6. independent voters
7. open primary
8. secret ballots
9. split ticket
10. straight ticket

Understanding Main Ideas
1. a
2. d

SECTION 4
Organizing Information
(1) Citizens cast their vote for president. (2) Electors gather and cast state's electoral votes. (3) Electoral votes sent to president *pro tempore*. (4) Electoral votes are counted. (5) Discover that no candidate receives majority of votes. (6) House of Representatives chooses president.

Evaluating Information
1. T
2. T
3. T
4. F
5. F

Reviewing Facts
1. party platform
2. popular vote
3. presidential primaries
4. electoral college
5. favorite sons or daughters
6. electoral vote
7. Electors

Chapter 11
SECTION 1
Organizing Information
Clockwise from top—endorsements from famous people; name-calling; candidates describe themselves as plain, hardworking citizens; bandwagon; using words that sound good but have little meaning; card stacking.

Evaluating Information
1. F
2. T
3. F
4. F
5. T
6. T

Reviewing Facts
1. Revealed propaganda
2. poll
3. Public opinion
4. propaganda
5. mass media
6. Concealed propaganda

SECTION 2
Organizing Information
Answers will vary, but students should recognize the following: lobbyists argue in support of bills they favor and against bills they oppose; they supply information; they testify at committee hearings.

Evaluating Information
1. T
2. F
3. F
4. F
5. T
6. F
7. T
8. T

Understanding Main Ideas
1. b
2. d
3. d

SECTION 3
Organizing Information
Answers will vary, but students might include the following: ring doorbells or make phone calls to inform voters; encourage friends and family members to vote; distribute literature; address, stuff, and mail envelopes; baby-sit so parents can go to vote.

Evaluating Information
1. F
2. T
3. F
4. F
5. F
6. T
7. F
8. F
9. T
10. T
11. F
12. T
13. T
14. T

Chapter 12
SECTION 1
Organizing Information
Population has increased; cost of living is rising; government provides many programs and services; money is spent on national defense; debt; number of people receiving benefits has increased.

Evaluating Information
1. F
2. T
3. T
4. F
5. T
6. T
7. F
8. T
9. T
10. F

Reviewing Facts
1. fees
2. fines
3. national debt
4. Revenue
5. Interest
6. bond

SECTION 2
Organizing Information
Collected on most products sold; collected on "luxury" services and goods; property tax; collected on portion of estate inherited by an individual; gift tax; collected on earnings of individuals and companies; collected from all the wealth a person leaves his or her heirs; Social Security tax.

Reviewing Facts
1. progressive tax
2. real property
3. tariff
4. exemption
5. profit
6. regressive tax
7. taxable income
8. personal property
9. deductions

Evaluating Information
1. T
2. T
3. F
4. F
5. T
6. T
7. F
8. T

SECTION 3
Organizing Information
Executive departments estimate money to be spent; president and OMB create budget; Senate and House of Representatives receive budget; Congress makes changes to budget; president approves final budget.

Evaluating Information
1. T
2. F
3. T
4. F
5. F
6. T
7. T
8. F

Understanding Main Ideas
1. b
2. d
3. c
4. c

Chapter 13
SECTION 1
Organizing Information
Delayed marriage—growing acceptance of singlehood as a way of life; finish educations first; increase in couples who live together without being married. Two-income families —economic necessity; women want to put skills into use. Single-parent families—divorce. Remarriages—people who have divorced remarry and combine families.

Evaluating Information
1. T
2. F
3. T
4. F
5. F
6. T
7. F
8. T

Reviewing Facts
1. remarried
2. two-income family
3. single-parent families
4. blended families
5. delayed marriage

SECTION 2
Organizing Information
Reasons a court may intervene in a marriage—nonsupport, physical abuse, desertion.
Reasons a court may intervene in a home with children—emotional abuse, physical abuse, sexual abuse.

Evaluating Information
1. F
2. T
3. F
4. F
5. T
6. T

Understanding Main Ideas
1. d
2. b
3. c
4. b

SECTION 3
Organizing Information
House or apartment payments, food, insurance, telephone bills, credit card payments, clothing, medical expenses, entertainment, savings.

Evaluating Information

1. T		**8.** T	
2. T		**9.** T	
3. F		**10.** T	
4. T		**11.** T	
5. F		**12.** F	
6. F		**13.** F	
7. T		**14.** F	

Chapter 14

SECTION 1
Organizing Information

Pros—necessary for democracy to operate effectively; necessary for democratic society to have citizens who can read and write; would ensure that poor children would be educated as well as rich children.

Cons—Poor children couldn't work to make money for families. People did not want to pay money to educate other people's children. It would decrease private school enrollment.

Evaluating Information

1. F	**5.** F
2. F	**6.** T
3. T	**7.** F
4. T	**8.** T

Reviewing Facts

1. university
2. community colleges
3. colleges
4. Mainstreaming
5. graduate school

SECTION 2
Organizing Information

Use study guides in the book. Note title, section headings, and subheadings in chapter. Note topic sentences and summarize paragraphs. Reread text and make notes. Answer questions at the end of each section. Use an index-card file.

Evaluating Information

1. F	**5.** F
2. T	**6.** T
3. F	**7.** T
4. T	

Understanding Main Ideas

1. c	**3.** d
2. a	**4.** c

SECTION 3
Reviewing Facts

1. Prejudice	**5.** creativity
2. Motivation	**6.** habit
3. conditioning	**7.** experience
4. critical thinking	**8.** insight

Evaluating Information

1. T	**8.** F
2. F	**9.** F
3. T	**10.** T
4. F	**11.** T
5. T	**12.** T
6. T	**13.** T
7. T	**14.** F

Chapter 15

SECTION 1
Organizing Information

Answers may vary.

Rural farm community—grow crops based on climate. Small country town—population is less than 2,500, usually located near open farmland. Suburbs—town, village, or community located on the outskirts of a city. Urban area—boroughs, towns, villages, and cities of 2,500 or more people. Metropolitan area—cities and their surrounding towns and suburbs.

Evaluating Information

1. F	**6.** T
2. T	**7.** T
3. T	**8.** F
4. T	**9.** T
5. F	**10.** F

Reviewing Facts

1. crossroads
2. megalopolis
3. metropolitan area

SECTION 2
Organizing Information

Answers will vary—conversation, telephones, e-mail, Internet, radios, televisions, writing, newspaper

Evaluating Information

1. T	**4.** F
2. T	**5.** T
3. T	**6.** F

Understanding Main Ideas

1. d	**3.** a
2. c	**4.** c

SECTION 3
Classifying Information

1. b, c	**6.** d
2. c	**7.** c
3. b	**8.** b, c
4. d	**9.** d
5. a	**10.** d

Evaluating Information

1. F	**8.** T
2. T	**9.** F
3. T	**10.** T
4. T	**11.** T
5. F	**12.** T
6. F	**13.** F
7. T	**14.** T

Chapter 16

SECTION 1
Organizing Information

Poverty, illegal drug use, permissive society, urbanization

Evaluating Information

1. F	**5.** F
2. T	**6.** F
3. F	**7.** T
4. T	**8.** T

Classifying Information

1. a	**6.** c
2. b	**7.** b
3. d	**8.** a
4. b	**9.** d
5. e	**10.** a

SECTION 2
Reviewing Facts

1. probable cause
2. community policing
3. plea bargain
4. criminal justice system
5. parole

6. acquitted
7. arraigned
8. defense
9. prosecution

Evaluating Information

1. T	**4.** T
2. F	**5.** T
3. F	**6.** F

Understanding Main Ideas

1. a	**3.** c
2. c	**4.** d

SECTION 3
Organizing Information

Do not use drugs. Stay in school. Have the courage to say "no" when friends suggest illegal acts. Participate in many physical activities and interesting hobbies.

Evaluating Information

1. F	**8.** T
2. F	**9.** F
3. F	**10.** F
4. T	**11.** T
5. T	**12.** T
6. T	**13.** T
7. F	**14.** F

Chapter 17

SECTION 1
Organizing Information

Command economy—Government owns almost all of the capital, tools, and production equipment. Government tells factories what and how much to produce.
Mixed economy—Both citizens and government control the economy.
Free economy—Government has no control over the economy at all.
Traditional economy—Production is based on customs and traditions.

Evaluating Information

1. T	**4.** T
2. F	**5.** F
3. T	

Reviewing Facts

1. Capitalism
2. conglomerate

3. law of demand

4. market economy

5. invest

6. free competition

7. monopoly

8. profit motive

9. merger

SECTION 2
Reviewing Facts

1. dividends

2. common stock

3. partnerships

4. sole proprietorships

5. preferred stock

6. Nonprofit organizations

7. corporation

8. stockholders

9. Stocks

Evaluating Information

1. T		**5.** T	
2. F		**6.** T	
3. F		**7.** F	
4. F		**8.** T	

Classifying Information

1. a		**6.** e	
2. b		**7.** b	
3. d		**8.** c	
4. c		**9.** c	
5. a		**10.** d	

SECTION 3
Organizing Information

Answers may vary—Government acts as referee to ensure that big corporations do not destroy competition from small businesses; protects a person's rights to own private property and buy and sell in a free market; protects workers' health and safety; prevents pollution; protects buyers; ensures employers cannot discriminate; provides information to managers; provides loans.

Evaluating Information

1. F		**6.** F	
2. T		**7.** T	
3. T		**8.** T	
4. F		**9.** T	
5. T		**10.** T	

Understanding Main Ideas

1. d

2. b

3. d

4. d

Chapter 18

SECTION 1
Organizing Information

Machine tools—machinery built to produce parts that are exactly the same
Interchangeable parts—parts being exactly alike so they may be changed and switched
Division of labor—job divided into several tasks among various workers, each worker being a specialist at a certain part of the job

Evaluating Information

1. T		**5.** F	
2. F		**6.** T	
3. T		**7.** F	
4. T		**8.** T	

Reviewing Facts

1. division of labor

2. assembly line

3. gross domestic product

4. Interchangeable parts

5. Mass production

6. Machine tools

SECTION 2
Organizing Information

Railroads; decrease; many tracks and trains in poor condition, not very fast
Air transportation; increase; none mentioned
Highway system; increase; bad roads and causes traffic jams, accidents, air pollution, and heavy use of gasoline and oil

Reviewing Facts

1. brand name

2. one-price system

3. wholesaler

4. Distribution

5. mass marketing

6. Retailers or Retail stores

7. Self-service

8. Advertising

9. Standard packaging

Evaluating Information

1. T	**4.** F
2. T	**5.** F
3. T	**6.** T

SECTION 3
Organizing Information

Cash, charge accounts, installment plan

Evaluating Information

1. F	**6.** F
2. F	**7.** T
3. F	**8.** F
4. T	**9.** T
5. T	**10.** F

Understanding Main Ideas

1. a
2. b
3. c
4. d

Chapter 19
SECTION 1
Organizing Information

cash, check, debit card, charge account, credit card

Evaluating Information

1. T	**6.** T
2. F	**7.** T
3. F	**8.** F
4. F	**9.** F
5. T	**10.** F

Reviewing Facts

1. Credit cards
2. Long-term credit
3. Money
4. check
5. short-term credit
6. currency
7. Debit cards
8. creditors
9. Bankruptcy

SECTION 2
Organizing Information

Commercial banks—offer checking, savings, and NOW accounts, and loans and credit cards; help to manage retirement funds, property, and investments; insured by FDIC. Savings and loan associations—offer home mortgage loans; checking, savings, and NOW accounts; and credit cards; insured by FDIC. Savings banks—offer home loans and savings and checking accounts; insured by FDIC. Credit unions—offer loans, checking and savings accounts, retirement planning, and credit cards; not insured by FDIC.

Evaluating Information

1. T	**6.** F
2. T	**7.** F
3. T	**8.** T
4. T	**9.** F
5. F	**10.** T

Understanding Main Ideas

1. c	**3.** a
2. b	**4.** d

SECTION 3
Classifying Information

1. a	**4.** a
2. b	**5.** a
3. a	**6.** b

Evaluating Information

1. F	**8.** T
2. T	**9.** F
3. F	**10.** T
4. T	**11.** T
5. T	**12.** T
6. F	**13.** F
7. T	**14.** F

Reviewing Facts

1. Money-market funds
2. brokers
3. stock exchange
4. Certificates of deposit (CDs)
5. Mutual funds

SECTION 4

Organizing Information

Answers may vary but can include private insurance, life insurance, disability income and health insurance, property and liability insurance, and social insurance.

Evaluating Information

1.	T	5.	T
2.	F	6.	F
3.	F	7.	T
4.	T	8.	F

Reviewing Facts

1. social insurance
2. Insurance
3. premium
4. Private insurance
5. beneficiary
6. Medicare

Chapter 20

SECTION 1

Organizing Information

Expansion—GDP increases, unemployment rate decreases, prices increase, profits increase. Contraction—GDP decreases, unemployment rate increases, prices decrease, profits decrease.

Evaluating Information

1.	F	6.	T
2.	F	7.	T
3.	F	8.	F
4.	T	9.	T
5.	T	10.	T

Reviewing Facts

1. depression
2. business cycle
3. contraction
4. expansion
5. Inflation
6. trough
7. costs of production
8. peak
9. recession

SECTION 2

Organizing Information

Circulation of too much money; banks issuing too many loans; government spending and borrowing; too little consumer saving and too much spending; decreased productivity in the United States relative to foreign countries.

Evaluating Information

1.	F	5.	F
2.	T	6.	T
3.	T	7.	T
4.	F	8.	T

Understanding Main Ideas

1.	c	3.	d
2.	b	4.	c

SECTION 3

Evaluating Information

1.	F	7.	T
2.	F	8.	T
3.	T	9.	F
4.	T	10.	F
5.	F	11.	F
6.	F	12.	F

Reviewing Facts

1. Blacklists
2. collective bargaining
3. labor unions
4. lockouts
5. strike
6. open shop
7. Picketing
8. job action
9. closed shop

Chapter 21

SECTION 1

Organizing Information

Traditional economy: based on customs and traditions

Command economy: government officials make economic plans for the country

Market economy: government plays no role at all in making economic decisions

Mixed economy: includes elements of traditional, command, and market economies

Evaluating Information

1. F
2. F
3. F
4. T
5. F

Reviewing Facts

1. law of supply
2. Human resources
3. producer
4. law of demand
5. Supply
6. Capital resources
7. circular-flow model
8. Demand
9. capital goods

SECTION 2
Organizing Information

Expansion, peak, contraction, trough

Evaluating Information

1. F
2. T
3. T
4. F
5. F
6. F
7. T
8. F
9. T
10. T

Understanding Main Ideas

1. c
2. c
3. a

SECTION 3
Organizing Information

Government investments: enable producers and consumers to participate in the economy

Government regulation: protects workers and consumers, limits negative affects, and encourages competition
Fiscal policy: spending, taxing, and borrowing
Monetary policy: promotes economic growth, determines amount of money available in the economy at any given time

Reviewing Facts

1. tax incentive
2. reserve requirement
3. Tight-money policy
4. infrastructure
5. easy-money policy
6. discount rate
7. Open-market operations

Evaluating Information

1. T
2. T
3. T
4. F
5. T
6. F
7. F
8. F

SECTION 4
Organizing Information

Infant industries: free trade supporters believe that protection will weaken infant industries; protectionists argue that infant industries need protection from foreign competition.

Job protection: free trade supporters claim that protectionism costs American jobs; protectionists say that reducing foreign competition creates more jobs at home.

Standard of living: free trade supporters believe that high wages and high standard of living do not require trade barriers; protectionists claim that trade barrier maintain high wages and a high standard of living.

Specialization: free trade supporters believe that competition forces businesses to produce the best product possible; protectionists argue that free trade leads businesses to overspecialize.

Evaluating Information

1. F
2. F
3. T
4. T
5. F

Reviewing Facts

1. trade-off
2. interdependence
3. absolute advantage
4. specialize
5. Opportunity cost
6. trade barrier
7. comparative advantage

Chapter 22

SECTION 1
Organizing Information

Various reasons: desire for high income, helping others, meeting basic needs, high living standard, career advancement, challenge, comfortable routine.

Evaluating Information

1. F	6. F
2. T	7. T
3. T	8. T
4. T	9. F
5. F	10. T

Understanding Main Ideas

1. c
2. d

SECTION 2
Organizing Information

Answers may vary but may include the following: people in charge of large businesses; sales workers; professionals; lab technicians, physical therapists; electrician, plumber.

Evaluating Information

1. F	5. T
2. F	6. T
3. T	7. T
4. F	8. T

Reviewing Facts

1. Automation
2. professionals
3. blue-collar workers
4. apprenticeship
5. Agribusinesses
6. White-collar workers
7. Technicians
8. operators
9. laborers

SECTION 3
Organizing Information

Answers will vary, but may include deliver mail; care for war veterans; protect against counterfeiting; run national parks; forecast weather; inspect food and medicine.

Evaluating Information

1. T	8. T
2. T	9. T
3. T	10. T
4. F	11. F
5. F	12. T
6. F	13. T
7. F	14. T

SECTION 4
Organizing Information

Answers will vary.

Evaluating Information

1. F	5. F
2. T	6. F
3. F	7. F
4. T	8. T

Understanding Main Ideas

1. a
2. d

SECTION 5
Organizing Information

Answers will vary.

Evaluating Information

1. T	5. F
2. T	6. T
3. T	7. T
4. F	

Reviewing Facts

1. Interpersonal skills
2. aptitude tests
3. perceptual skills
4. Motor skills

Chapter 23
SECTION 1
Organizing Information

Goals: maintain national security; support democracy; promote world peace; provide aid to people in need; establish free and open trade.

Evaluating Information

1. T	5. T
2. F	6. T
3. T	7. T
4. F	

Reviewing Facts

1. diplomatic corps
2. Interdependence
3. Diplomatic recognition
4. Couriers
5. alliance
6. executive agreement

SECTION 2
Reviewing Facts
1. Foreign aid
2. Free trade
3. balance of trade
4. Exports
5. summit
6. Newly industrialized countries
7. Imports
8. Trade deficits

Evaluating Information
1. F	5. F
2. F	6. T
3. T	7. F
4. T	8. T

Understanding Main Ideas
1. c	3. c
2. b	4. d

SECTION 3
Organizing Information

General Assembly: discusses, debates, and recommends solutions to problems

Security Council: responsible for peace-keeping

International Court of Justice: court that hears disputes related to international law

Economic and Social Council: improves the lives of the world's people

Trusteeship Council: helped non-self-governing colonies at the end of WWII

Secretariat: manages day-to-day activities of UN and provides services to other UN divisions

Reviewing Facts
1. International Court of Justice
2. General Assembly
3. Security Council
4. United Nations

Evaluating Information
1. T	5. F
2. T	6. T
3. T	7. T
4. F	8. F

Chapter 24
SECTION 1
Organizing Information
Canada—Conflict: Disagreed over who controlled waterways. Result: Rush-Bagot Agreement

Latin America—Conflict: U.S. helped in settling boundary disputes, but became oppressive. Result: Good Neighbor Policy

Germany—Conflict: Germans attacked U.S. ships. Result: WWI

Japan—Conflict: Japanese bombed Pearl Harbor. Result: WWII

Evaluating Information
1. T	6. F
2. T	7. T
3. F	8. T
4. T	9. T
5. T	10. F

Reviewing Facts
1. doctrine	4. neutrality
2. corollary	5. dollar diplomacy
3. Isolationism	

SECTION 2
Reviewing Facts
1. balance of power	5. glasnost
2. Communism	6. Satellite nations
3. containment	7. Perestroika
4. limited war	8. Détente

Evaluating Information
1. T	6. T
2. F	7. T
3. F	8. T
4. F	9. F
5. T	10. T

Understanding Main Ideas
1. a	3. b
2. a	4. c

SECTION 3
Classifying Information
1. c	6. b
2. b	7. d
3. d	8. b
4. a	9. a
5. d	10. c

Evaluating Information

1.	T	7.	T
2.	F	8.	T
3.	T	9.	F
4.	T	10.	F
5.	T	11.	T
6.	F	12.	F

Chapter 25

SECTION 1
Organizing Information
Innermost circle—downtown
Middle circle—inner residential sector and suburbs
Outer circle—rural–urban fringe

Evaluating Information

1.	F	5.	T
2.	T	6.	T
3.	F	7.	T
4.	F	8.	T

Reviewing Facts
1. Public housing projects
2. Mass transit
3. Urban-renewal programs
4. Zoning laws
5. Homelessness
6. Building codes

SECTION 2
Organizing Information
Answers may include African Americans, Hispanics, American Indians, Vietnamese, Muslims and persons with disabilities.

Reviewing Facts
1. civil rights movement
2. ethnic group
3. Minority groups
4. Discrimination
5. boycott
6. demonstration
7. civil disobedience
8. Dissent

Evaluating Information

1.	T	4.	T
2.	T	5.	F
3.	F		

SECTION 3
Organizing Information
Drug abuse—Refrain from drug use.
Alcohol abuse—Refrain from alcohol.
Smoking—Refrain from smoking.
AIDS—Do not have unprotected sex or share needles.
Accidents—Wear seatbelts; do not be careless.

Evaluating Information

1.	T	8.	T
2.	T	9.	F
3.	F	10.	F
4.	F	11.	T
5.	T	12.	T
6.	F	13.	T
7.	T	14.	F

Chapter 26

SECTION 1
Organizing Information
Bottom to top: plankton, shrimp, fish, humans

Evaluating Information

1.	T	5.	F
2.	F	6.	T
3.	F	7.	F
4.	F	8.	T

Reviewing Facts

1.	Erosion	5.	Fertilizers
2.	Organic farming	6.	ecology
3.	ecosystem	7.	Pesticides
4.	Desertification		

SECTION 2
Organizing Information
Air pollution—Stop using CFCs.
Water pollution—Treat sewage; don't litter; conserve water.
Ground pollution—Recycle; don't litter.

Reviewing Facts
1. Acid rain
2. Recycling
3. Pollution
4. renewable resource
5. Landfills
6. hydrologic cycle
7. smog
8. greenhouse effect
9. ozone layer

Understanding Main Ideas

1. d   **2.** a

SECTION 3
Organizing Information

Renewable resources—trees, plants
Nonrenewable resources—minerals, metals, ores, fossil fuels

Evaluating Information

1. F	**8.** T
2. F	**9.** T
3. T	**10.** T
4. T	**11.** F
5. T	**12.** T
6. F	**13.** F
7. F	**14.** T

SECTION 4
Organizing Information

National Environmental Policy Act; Clean Air Acts; water pollution control acts; Resource Conservation and Recovery Act; Wild and Scenic Rivers Act; Endangered Species Acts

Evaluating Information

1. F	**4.** T
2. T	**5.** T
3. T	**6.** F

Understanding Main Ideas

1. a	**3.** c
2. d	**4.** d